THE PATTE
REVEALED

BY MOREH MIYKAEL QORBANYAHU
AKA B. MICHAEL LONG

THE PATTERN OF ADAM REVEALED

By Moreh Miykael Qorbanyahu
aka
B. Michael Long

Edition Notice

Title: The Pattern of Adam Revealed
Author: Miykael Qorbanyahu aka B. Michael Long
Publisher: Long Life Enterprises LLC
Cover Design by B. Michael Long
ISBN: 9798329837186

Long Life Enterprises: enterpriselonglife@outlook.com
For Booking B. Michael: bmichaelspeaks@outlook.com
Website: www.bmichaelspeaks.com

CONTENTS

PREFACE

It was in 1997, as a student-athlete on the UMaine Black Bear football team during my redshirt junior year, that my life was completely transformed. The catalyst took place two years earlier during an encounter with my mortality resulting from a bout with a cannabis-induced anxiety-attack. After that experience, I intentionally embarked on an extensive journey on a search for meaning in the worlds of philosophy and spirituality. '97 was the year I determined to "go to heaven" as it was a time when I finally found a center point within. In April that year while on spring break, I was introduced by one of my oldest friends to, who I knew at that time, my "Lord and Savior, Jesus Christ."

Prior to that, however, my first twenty-one years of life were, at best, happy-go-lucky, random, whimsical, erratic and entirely circumstantial relative to my poor decision-making skills and reactionary mode of operation in life. At that time, I was playing tic-tac-toe and not chess. When I experienced my rebirth, however, I decided to become more intentional and decisive with my decisions and actions, though it was and still is an everyday journey that requires me to find myself present in the moment in order to connect with the now and beyond.

It was also during this time that I set my heart to intensively study the Scriptures. I made this my focus as I remember sitting in my grandparents living room during that same spring break year reading 2 Thessalonians 2.9-12 which speaks of the deception of the lawless one and the delusion sent by Elohim to those who reject the truth. The words from that text impacted me to such a degree that at that moment I made it my mission to "*study to show [myself] approved as worker who is not ashamed, rightly handling the word of Truth*" (2 Timothy 2.15).

Also that same year, due to the fourth and final injury I suffered from playing college football, I had come to experience yet another season of solitude. This time, however, unlike the other times, I invested in my soul and did the shadow work. I also found myself more involved in extra-curricular activities. One such activity was Campus Crusade for Christ, and it was there that I met one of the most influential individuals I had come across during my collegiate years. His name was Doug. As my spiritual advisor and mentor, he introduced to me many new ideas relative to spiritual consciousness and Scriptural knowledge. In fact, one in particular has stuck with me over the course of my journey and serves as the foundational premise of this work. Doug showed me how the Scriptures reveal that humanity has a threefold purpose which can be found in Genesis 1.26. According to the passage, the purpose of humanity is to:

1. ***reflect*** the image and likeness of YaH,
2. ***reign*** over self and creation and
3. ***reproduce*** the image and likeness of YaH, spiritually, intellectually and physically.

Inspired by the lesson that I learned from my guy Doug, *The Pattern of Adam Revealed (TPOAR): Innerstanding Humanity's Heavenly Purpose*, will explore the threefold role of humanity, bringing into focus the people of the covenant, who have been elected by YaH to reflect the "image and likeness" of Elohim on Earth and manifest the Shekinah Presence of the King of kings.

Before proceeding forward, however, it is essential to note that with my first book, *The Kingdom Within* (TKW): *Exploring Torah-Based Governance and Prophetic Messianic Redemption*, I decided to zoom out and take a macroscopic view of creation, beginning with the main idea of the Scriptures, the Kingdom of Heaven on Earth. By exploring Torah-based governance, leadership, personal transformation and prophetic Messianic redemption, the purpose of TKW was to initiate, inspire, edify and encourage readers to either launch or deepen their journey on the path to manifest the Kingdom Within[1].

Now with TPOAR I have decided to zoom in, focusing on the microcosm of creation epitomized by humanity within this grand design—the individual and our collective journey towards fulfilling its heavenly assigned purpose as envoys and emissaries for the Kingdom of Heaven on Earth. At the heart of this exploration lies the profound principle of humanity being created in the "image and likeness" of Elohim. This phrase, deeply rooted in the Hebrew Scriptures, has been the subject of theological inquiry and mystical contemplation for millennia. It is now my intention to provide a cultural, historical and linguistic insight into the mysteries of the Scriptures and the depths of our being for the purpose of unlocking our greatest potential to become a reflection of the Majesty on High here on Earth in the Spirit of Messiah Yeshua who told his disciples, "*He who has seen Me has seen the Father*..." (John 14.9).

In Genesis 1:26-27, we encounter the foundational declaration that humanity is created in the image and likeness of Elohim. This heavenly imprint, this supernatural ancestry, this metaphysical inheritance carries profound implications for our understanding of self and our relationship with the Most High, YHWH El Elyon - the Elohim of Abraham, Isaac and Jacob. When considering these dynamics, they further beg questions such as:

- What is the purpose of humanity and life itself?
- What does it truly mean to bear the image and likeness of the Creator?
- How do we live out this heavenly calling in our everyday lives?

These questions frame the purpose of TPOAR which is to present the Scriptural paradigm and the methods of achieving the threefold purpose of humanity. With TPOAR, I am seeking to unravel these questions, drawing upon the native soil and rich tapestry of Torah principles, rabbinic teachings, Kabbalistic[2] insights and Messianic perspectives. Through an exploration of Israel's ancient wisdom and contemporary scholarship, we will embark on a journey of inner discovery and spiritual awakening, uncovering the hidden truths encoded within the Scriptures and ourselves.

This work will also delve into the multifaceted dimensions of humanity's highest purpose, examining the ethical, spiritual and practical implications of bearing the image and likeness of Elohim. We will explore the concept of heaven's reflection, the transformative power of spiritual embodiment, and the sacred responsibility entrusted to humanity as stewards of creation.

TPOAR will also address the objectives and goals that arise on the path towards fulfilling our heavenly calling. From self-mastery and victory over sin to the manifestation of Messianic consciousness, we will present the principles that are a part of humanity's journey towards wholeness and holiness.

Ultimately, TPOAR is a call to innerstanding—a journey that involves embarking upon the process of deep introspection, self-discovery and spiritual growth that leads us towards the fulfillment of our highest potential. It is an invitation to awaken to the divine spark within, to embrace our role as co-creators with YaH and to participate in the ongoing revelation for the manifestation of YaH's presence in the world.

Let us enter now the inner sanctum of life.

In Messiah, Moreh Miykael Qorbanyahu aka B. Michael Long

PROLOGUE: THE PATTERN

The Hebrew word *tabnit* (תַּבְנִית) holds a significant place for comprehending the biblical principles of divine patterns and archetypes. The term, which can be translated into English as *pattern*, *form* or *model*, appears in key scriptural passages that reveal profound insights into YaH's intentions for creation and redemption. Its implicit use in Genesis 1:26 and then explicitly in Exodus 25:9 provides a foundational understanding of humanity's purpose and the sacred design and intent of the Tabernacle relative to its redemptive functions.

Genesis 1:26 states, "*Then Elohim said, 'Let us make man in our image, after our likeness. And let them have dominion over the fish of the sea and over the birds of the heavens and over the livestock and over all the earth and over every creeping thing that creeps on the earth.*'"

Here, the concept of *tabnit* is implied in the idea of humanity being created in the image (צֶלֶם/*tzelem*) and likeness (דְּמוּת/*demut*) of Elohim. Although the word tabnit is not directly used in this verse, the notion of a divine pattern is central. The creation of humanity according to a divine model suggests that humans are meant to reflect YaH's attributes and character, to possess YaH's perception and intellect[3]. This reflection is not just physical but encompasses moral, spiritual and relational dimensions.

In Genesis 1:26, the creation of humanity in the image of Elohim suggests that humans are designed according to a heavenly prototype. This pattern includes:

1. **Moral Attributes**

Humans are endowed with the capacity for holiness, righteousness, justice, love and mercy, mirroring YaH's moral nature.

2. **Spiritual Capacity**

Humas have the ability to commune, in Spirit and Truth with Elohim, as well as worship and experience spiritual renewal as part of this divine imprint.

3. **Relational Aspect**

Humans are created to live in relationships that reflect divine harmony and unity, echoing the relational nature of the Most High Elohim.

These three aspects of the pattern sets up the structure of both humanity and the Tabernacle/Temple construct. The three-dimensional constitution of humanity and the houses of worship both capture the divine essence and intended unification of spirit, soul and body. Scripture provides humanity with the instructions of how to properly conduct the structures in order to make the dwelling places suitable for the Shekinah Presence of YaH to indwell them.

Giving context to the instructions to manifest the Presence of YaH, Exodus 25:9 states, "*Exactly as I show you concerning the pattern (tabnit) of the Tabernacle*, *and of all its furniture*, *so you shall make it*."

In this context, tabnit refers explicitly to the divine blueprint given to Moses for constructing the Tabernacle. This structure was to be a physical representation of heavenly realities, serving as a place where YaH's presence would dwell among His people. The Tabernacle was meticulously designed to reflect spiritual truths and heavenly archetypes.

The use of tabnit in Exodus 25:9 underscores a few key principles:

1. **Heavenly Origin**

The design of the Tabernacle is not a human invention but a revelation from YaH, reflecting heavenly realities.

2. **Exactness and Fidelity**

Moses was instructed to follow the pattern precisely, indicating that the physical structure was to be a faithful representation of a higher, spiritual reality which we are to manifest on Earth.

3. **Symbolic Elements**

Every aspect of the Tabernacle—from its measurements to its materials and furnishings—had symbolic significance, teaching spiritual truths about YaH's nature, human sin and redemption.

The use of tabnit in these two contexts reveals a deeper connection between humanity and the Tabernacle:

1. **Reflecting Shekinah Presence**

Just as the Tabernacle was designed to house YaH's presence and reflect His esteem, humanity was created to reflect YaH's image and serve as His representatives on earth.

2. **Mediating Shekinah Presence**

The Tabernacle served as the place where YaH and humans could meet, prefiguring the ultimate union of immortality and humanity in the person of Yeshua the Messiah. Similarly, humans are called to be vessels of YaH's presence, mediating His love and truth to the world.

3. **Pattern of Redemption**

The meticulous design of the Tabernacle points to the order and intentionality of YaH's redemptive plan.

Likewise, the creation of humanity in YaH's image and likeness signifies a purposeful design, calling humans to live out their heavenly ordained vocation in alignment with YaH's will.

Rabbinic tradition also offers further insights into the concept of "tabnit" and its implications. Conceptually, the following ideas are articulated within the body of literature present in the tradition:

1. **Mishnaic Interpretation**

The Mishnah interprets Genesis 1:26 as highlighting the unique and unparalleled dignity of humanity, created in the image and likeness of Elohim, emphasizing that each person possesses inherent worth and an eternal spark. This interpretation underscores the ethical imperative to treat every individual with respect and justice, reflecting the divine image in our interactions.

2. **Talmudic Commentary**

The Talmud (Menachot 29b) discusses the intricate details given to Moses for the Tabernacle, emphasizing the importance of following YaH's exact instructions. This reflects the principle that earthly worship must symmetrically align with YaH's heavenly instructions given to Moses in order to be effective and pleasing to YaH.

On a deeper, symbolic level Kabbalistic teachings further delve into the significance of tabnit, providing its readers and practitioners with more profound insights and applications into the mysteries:

1. **Sefirotic Structure**:

In Kabbalah, the Tabernacle is seen in light of the Tree of life diagram and as a microcosm of the sefirotic structure of the universe, embodying divine attributes and serving as a point of connection between the finite and the infinite.

2. **Adam Kadmon**:

The concept of Adam Kadmon (Primordial Man) in Kabbalistic thought represents the ultimate "tabnit" or archetypal pattern of humanity, embodying the perfect heavenly image and serving as the template for all creation.

Understanding tabnit enriches our appreciation of the intricate relationship between divine intention and human vocation. It challenges us to live according to the heavenly patterns revealed in Scripture, embodying YaH's righteousness, justice and love in every aspect of our lives. As we strive to reflect the image of Elohim, we participate in the unfolding of YaH's redemptive plan, bringing light and order into a world marred by darkness and chaos.

From a Messianic perspective, the concept of tabnit finds its ultimate fulfillment in Yeshua the Messiah. Yeshua is the perfect image and likeness of Elohim, "t*he exact representation of His being*" (Hebrews 1:3). In Colossians 1:15, Paul writes, "*He is the image of the invisible Elohim, the firstborn of all creation.*" Yeshua embodies the heavenly tabnit, perfectly reflecting YaH's image, likeness, character, attributes, perception and intellect all for the sake of fulfilling Its purposes.

Moreover, Yeshua is also the epitome of the true Tabernacle; the dwelling place of Elohim among humanity. In John 1:14, it is written, "*and the Word became flesh and dwelt* (tabernacled) *among us, and we have seen his esteem, esteem as of the only Son from the Father, full of favor and truth.*" Yeshua's incarnation signifies the manifestation of the heavenly pattern in human form, opening the door for us to enter in the Name of YHWH which gives us access to the dimension between heaven and earth, enabling humanity to experience YaH's presence in a tangible, sensorial way.

The concept of tabnit carries profound cosmological implications for our understanding of Creator, creation, humanity, our place in it and redemption. As beings created in the heavenly image, we are called to reflect YaH's character and fulfill His purposes on earth. This involves cultivating virtues such as holiness, justice, compassion and humility, as well as exercising wise and righteous stewardship over creation.

Additionally, the pattern of the Tabernacle and its fulfillment in Yeshua points to the transformative power of YaH's presence. Just as the Tabernacle was a sacred space where YaH dwelt among His people, so too are our lives to be sanctuaries of the Shekinah Presence. By aligning ourselves with the divine pattern revealed in Yeshua, we become living tabernacles, vessels through which YaH's light and love can shine into the world. Embracing this concept challenges us to live in alignment with YaH's purposes, embodying Its virtues and manifesting the Shekinah Presence in our daily lives. The Presence of YaH in our lives, resulting from our self-abnegation and entering the Covenant of Torah observance, causes us to be agents of change, representing the manifestation of the new humanity, or the Second Adam, that Rabbi Sha'ul of Tarsus speaks of in 1 Corinthians 15.45.

UNDERSTANDING ADAM

With the idea of the tabernacle's pattern introduced, let us now turn our attention to the connection of the principle of pattern relative to the ideas pregnant with the Hebrew words "Adam" (אָדָם) and "Adamah" (אֲדָמָה). These two nouns are deeply intertwined and connected to the Tabernacle and Temple as they carry significant cosmological and spiritual meanings that illuminate humanity's origin, purpose and destiny. With one of the intents of this book, it is with the understanding of these terms in relation to Genesis 1:26 and their correlation to Exodus 25:9 that provides us with a richer comprehension of the scriptural narrative and its implications for human identity and our service to YaH and creation.

In Genesis 1:26 the term "Adam" signifies collective humanity, reflecting both the individual and corporate reality of human beings created in the image and likeness of Elohim. The name "Adam" is etymologically linked to "Adamah," the Hebrew word for "ground" or "earth." This connection highlights humanity's body origin coming from the earth, as described in Genesis 2:7: "*Then YaH Elohim formed the man (Adam) out of the dust from the ground (Adamah) and breathed into his nostrils the breath of life, and the man became a living soul.*" This dual reference underscores both the material and spiritual components of human nature—formed from the earth and animated by the breath of YaH.

The correlation between Genesis 1:26 and Exodus 25:9 lies in the concept of divine patterns and blueprints. Just as humanity (Adam) is created in the divine image and likeness, the Tabernacle is designed according to a heavenly pattern. Both serve as reflections of divine realities: Adam embodies the divine image on earth, and the Tabernacle represents YaH's dwelling among His people.

Again, we read in Exodus 25:9 where Elohim instructs Moses, "*According to all that I show you, the pattern (תַּבְנִית) of the tabernacle and the pattern of all its furnishings, just so shall you make it*." The Tabernacle, as the dwelling place of YaH's presence, was to be constructed according to a divinely revealed blueprint. The intricate design and materials of the Tabernacle symbolized the ordered cosmos and the sacred relationship between YaH and humanity.

From a rabbinic perspective, the creation of Adam from the earth (Adamah) and in the image of YaH emphasizes the unique role of humanity in the divine order. The Mishnah, in Pirkei Avot 3:14, states, "*Beloved is man, for he was created in the image of Elohim. It is even a greater love that it was made known to him that he was created in the image of Elohim.*" This highlights blueprint, Adam's special status and responsibility of humans to reflect YaH's character and uphold His commandments.

Rabbinic teachings also draw parallels between the Tabernacle and the Garden of Eden. Just as the Garden was a place where YaH walked with Adam (Genesis 3:8), the Tabernacle was a place where YaH dwelled among the Israelites. Both represent ideal environments of YaH.

Interestingly, kabbalistic teachings delve into the deeper symbolic significance of Adam and Adamah. The Zohar, a foundational text of Kabbalah, interprets "Adam" as not merely the first human but as an archetypal figure representing the entire human race. In Zohar 1:23b, it states, "*The word 'Adam' (man) is composed of Aleph, Dalet, Mem. The Aleph represents the divine spark, Dalet represents the physical form, and Mem represents the flowing waters of wisdom.*"

Kabbalah also explores the concept of the "primordial Adam" (Adam Kadmon), an idealized human form that embodies the heavenly blueprint for creation. This corresponds to the divine pattern of the Tabernacle, which, according to Kabbalistic tradition, reflects the heavenly Temple and the divine order of the cosmos. The physical Tabernacle and the spiritual Adam Kadmon both serve as manifestations of divine thought and intention.

From a Messianic perspective, Yeshua is referred to as the "second Adam" (1 Corinthians 15:45), who restores what was lost through the first Adam's disobedience. Rabbi Sha'ul of Tarsus writes at 1 Corinthians 15.45, "So it is written: *'The first man Adam became a living being'; the last Adam, a life-giving spirit.*" This passage highlights Yeshua's role in bringing spiritual reinvigoration, renewal and restoration to humanity.

Yeshua's incarnation also parallels the concept of the Tabernacle. John 1:14 declares, "*The Word became flesh and made his dwelling (tabernacled) among us. We have seen his esteem, the esteem of the one and only Son, who came from the Father, full of favor and truth.*" Yeshua embodies the divine presence on earth, fulfilling the pattern of the Tabernacle and revealing the fullness of YaH's esteem and favor.

The Hebrew words "Adam" (אָדָם) and "Adamah" (אֲדָמָה) also encapsulate profound cosmological truths about humanity's creation, purpose and destiny. As beings formed from the earth and bearing the image and likeness of Elohim, we are called to reflect YaH's character and fulfill His purposes on earth. The Tabernacle, constructed according to a divine pattern, serves as a tangible reminder of YaH's desire to dwell among His people and the sacredness of our relationship with Him.

Through the rabbinic, kabbalistic and messianic perspectives, we gain a multifaceted understanding of these concepts, enriching our appreciation of the heavenly blueprint that shapes our identity and calling. By aligning ourselves with this pattern and embodying the principles of justice, compassion and holiness, we fulfill our role as reflections of YaH's image and vessels of His presence in the world.

With "The Pattern of Adam Revealed," we embark on a profound journey to uncover the Torah's blueprint embedded in the creation of humanity, exploring the rich tapestry of meaning behind the Hebrew words tabnit (תַּבְנִית) "Adam" (אָדָם) and "Adamah" (אֲדָמָה). From a rabbinic perspective, we delve into the sacred texts to understand humanity's unique role and responsibility as beings created in the image and likeness of Elohim. Through the lens of Kabbalah, we explore the mystical dimensions of our existence, revealing how the archetypal patterns of creation and the Tabernacle reflect deeper spiritual truths. From a Messianic viewpoint, we examine how Yeshua embodies and fulfills these patterns, restoring and perfecting the image of YaH in humanity.

As we journey through these pages, we will illuminate the connections between humanity's creation and the heavenly pattern of the Tabernacle, exploring how these themes are interwoven throughout Scripture. We will uncover how understanding these foundational principles can transform our lives, guiding us to embody Heaven's principles of justice, compassion and holiness. Through this exploration, we aim to rediscover our true nature, reclaim the heavenly image and likeness, and fulfill our calling to be vessels of YaH's presence and light in the world.

INTRODUCTION

"*The Pattern of Adam Revealed: Innerstanding Humanity's Heavenly Purpose*" is based on Genesis 1.26-28. This book embarks on a profound journey, not merely to understand the semantics of language, which we will do, but to also illuminate the timeless wisdom, associative thoughts and the applications found hidden within them. Genesis, with its enigmatic passages, endless genealogies and eternal instructions presents humanity with a heavenly mandate—a heavenly commission echoing throughout the ages: SELF-MASTERY [Genesis 4.6]! It is with this in mind that we embark on our mission to purify and incarnate this heavenly directive which resonates with spiritual significance and cosmic consequence, whose purpose pervades throughout the Scriptures pages, ultimately to penetrate our pineal gland and illuminate our entire being [Matthew 6.22].

For humanity, it is with this purpose defining passage from the first chapter of Genesis where we are shown not the actual individual, but the archetypal pattern for humanity; male and female united, which is the most powerful reflection of the image and likeness of Elohim (Ephesians 5.31-32). For it is written that "*male and female He created them. And Elohim blessed them and said to them, 'be fruitful and increase in number; fill the earth and subdue it. Rule over the fish in the sea and the birds in the sky and over every living creature that moves on the ground.*'"

This mandate, initially bestowed upon Adam, extends far beyond the realm of individuality, surface reading and literal interpretation. It speaks to the very essence of humanity's purpose and role as stewards of creation, entrusted with the sacred task of nurturing, mastering and harmonizing the cosmos. Here, in the union of scripture and spirituality, we find a profound resonance with the insights of modern science. Relative to the interconnectedness of all life, Quantum Physics (QP) espouses the Grand Unified Theory[4], which seeks to maintain the delicate balance of ecosystems, and the intricate patterns woven into the fabric of existence—as all echo the heavenly command to "*fill the earth and subdue it.*" For it is through mastery that creation will experience true proliferation and the harmony of oneness.

In the unfolding narrative of Genesis 1, Adam emerges not merely as an individual but as a symbol—an archetype embodying the image and likeness of YaH while simultaneously reflecting the sovereign rulership of Heaven on Earth. YaH's mandate of mastery for Adam is not one of domination but of stewardship—a call to cultivate a harmonious relationship with the natural order of the world and to nurture the flourishing development of all living beings. In this light, let us clearly comprehend that the directive to "*rule over*" is not an assertion of dominance, rather it is an invitation to exercise wisdom, compassion, self-mastery and reverence in our interactions with the Earth and its inhabitants.

To truly grasp this order, let us delve into the depths of this ancient text attributed to Moses. Once we open its pages, it is essential that we learn to transcend the boundaries of Western conventional interpretations and embrace an original Eastern, comprehensive, dynamic and circular understanding of the text that integrates the insights of both science and spirituality. For in the unveiling of the pattern of Adam, we discover not only humanity's purpose but also a blueprint for co-creating a more harmonious and sustainable world—a world where the heavenly mandate to "*be fruitful and multiply*" is realized not only in the proliferation of our species but in the flourishing of all life forms, in a symphony of interconnectedness and reverence for the sacredness of existence.

Not only this, according to a treatise called the Ethics of the Fathers, or Pirke Avot[5], the commandment to be fruitful and multiply also applies to the activity of "raising up many disciples," a decree issued by the elders of the Great Assembly known in Hebrew as the Beit Din, or the House of Judgment, which is more commonly known as the Sanhedrin. It is this imperative that truly fulfills the commandment of YaH pertaining to reproducing, as it is the recreation of the Mind (image) and Nature (likeness) of YaH in humanity that truly establishes the intent of this great commission. This consciousness was also echoed by the Master Rabbi Messiah Yeshua ben Yoseph when He orders His taught ones to "*go and make disciples of all nations, immersing them in the Name of the Father, Son and Holy Spirit, teaching them to guard all that I have commanded you (Matthew 28.19-20).*" Relative to the inner meaning of fruitfulness and multiplication, Yeshua knew full well that discipleship was a fulfillment of the commandment to be fruitful and multiply which our Father and King gave to the offspring of Adam in the beginning.

Additionally, Abraham, revered as the patriarch of the three monotheistic faiths of Judaism, Christianity, and Islam, stands as a towering figure in the biblical narrative, renowned for his unwavering faith, righteousness and spiritual leadership. From a scriptural perspective, Abraham's mastery in being fruitful and multiplying extends beyond mere biological descendants to his profound influence in leading countless souls to the teachings and ways of Torah. This becomes evident with **Genesis 22:17-18**, where YaH reaffirms His covenant with Abraham, promising, "*I will surely bless you, and I will surely multiply your offspring as the stars of heaven and as the sand that is on the seashore. And your offspring shall possess the gate of his enemies, and in your offspring shall all the nations of the earth be blessed, because you have obeyed my voice*." Abraham's obedience and faithfulness are highlighted as instrumental in the fulfillment of the divine promise, which extends beyond physical descendants to encompass spiritual progeny who would come to embody the values of Torah (Genesis 12.5).

It is significant to note at this point from an Israelite perspective that the purpose of the Torah[6], as considered in Deuteronomy 4:8-13, encompasses a multifaceted understanding that transcends mere legalism and encompasses spiritual enlightenment, ethical guidance and communal cohesion. In this powerful passage it is written, "*And what great nation is there, that has statutes and rules so righteous as all this Torah that I set before you today? Only take care, and guard your soul diligently, lest you forget the things that your eyes have seen, and lest they depart from your heart all the days of your life. Make them known to your children and your children's children—how on the day that you stood before YaH your Elohim at Horeb, YaH said to me, 'Gather the people to me, that I may let them hear My words, so that they may learn to fear Me all the days that they live on the earth, and that they may teach their children so.' And you came near and stood at the foot of the mountain, while the mountain burned with fire to the heart of heaven, wrapped in darkness, cloud, and gloom. Then YaH spoke to you out of the midst of the fire. You heard the sound of words but saw no form; there was only a voice.*"

This insight highlights the profound significance of Torah from an Israelite perspective, drawing upon the above mentioned passage to illuminate its multifaceted purpose. From this standpoint we comprehend that the Torah is not merely a collection of legalistic regulations but is regarded as a revelation from YaH that encompasses spiritual enlightenment, ethical guidance and communal cohesion. Torah is not merely a set of rules to be followed but is regarded as the very essence of YaH's instruction and guidance for humanity, intended to lead individuals and communities toward a life of righteousness, holiness and the fulfillment and manifestation of the Kingdom of Heaven on Earth.

From this passage, the Israelite tradition derives these three key purposes of the Torah:

1. Spiritual Enlightenment:

The Torah serves as a source of heavenly wisdom and guidance, illuminating the path of righteousness and holiness for individuals and communities. Through the study and observance of Torah, one can deepen their connection with the Most High, cultivate a sense of awe and reverence, and embark on a journey of spiritual growth and transformation. The encounter at Mount Sinai, described in Deuteronomy 4, symbolizes the revelation of Eternal truth and the transmission of Torah from YaH to humanity for our transformation into the heavenly beings of light known as the children of Elohim.

2. Ethical Guidance:

The Torah provides a comprehensive ethical framework for living a moral, set-apart and righteous life. Its statutes and instructions encompass various aspects of human behavior, addressing issues such as justice, compassion, honesty, and integrity. By adhering to the principles and commandments of Torah, individuals can uphold ethical standards and contribute to the betterment of society. The Torah's emphasis on justice and compassion reflects its far-reaching concern for the welfare of humanity.

3. Communal Cohesion:

The Torah also serves as a unifying force that binds the people of Israel and the household of faith together as a cohesive community. Through the shared study, observance and transmission of Torah, individuals and families connect with their heritage, strengthen their sense of identity and foster a collective sense of belonging. The commandment to "make them known to your children and your children's children" underscores the intergenerational transmission of Torah knowledge and values, ensuring the continuity of YaH's tradition given to Israel for cross-generational consciousness.

Overall, from the Scriptures perspective, the purpose of the Torah as depicted in Deuteronomy 4:8-13 is to serve as a divine blueprint for righteous living, guiding individuals and communities towards spiritual enlightenment, ethical conduct and communal cohesion. Through its teachings and commandments, the Torah offers a pathway to holiness, justice and fulfillment, inviting all who heed its call to walk in the ways of Elohim and to strive for the realization of a world imbued with divine wisdom and goodness.

The inner, Kabbalistic purpose of Torah transcends mere legalistic interpretations and delves into the mystical depths of Israel's tradition. Mentioned 14 times in 12 verses in the Hebrew scriptures in its root form, *qabal/* קָבַל, the inner teachings of Israel, means to receive, grasp or accept the hidden tradition and the hidden instruction of the Torah. As such, the principles of Kabbalah offer profound insights into the nature and purpose of Torah, understanding it not merely as a set of laws but as a heavenly blueprint for the universe and humanity's pathway to spiritual enlightenment.

In **1 Timothy 1:8-10**, it is written, "*We know that the Torah is good if one uses it properly. We also know that the law is made not for the righteous but for lawbreakers and rebels, the wicked and sinful, the unholy and irreligious, for those who kill their fathers or mothers, for murderers, for the sexually immoral, for those practicing homosexuality, for slave traders and liars and perjurers—and for whatever else is contrary to the sound doctrine.*" As revealed with this passage, the Torah serves as a corrective force, helping individuals to overcome their lower impulses, providing the instructions to elevate themselves to higher spiritual planes.

From the inner view of Israelite consciousness, the Torah is not simply a set of rules and regulations but the very essence of Heaven's wisdom and truth. Torah is the revealed will of YaH, encoded with the secrets of creation and the keys to unlocking spiritual enlightenment for entrance into the Kingdom. Torah is the heavenly light that illuminates the darkness of ignorance and guides humanity on the path of righteousness and holiness, as Yeshua taught[7], it is the **Way** (Psalm 119.1), the **Truth** (Psalm 119.142) and the **Life** (Deuteronomy 32.45-48).

With the inner Israelite tradition, the Torah is often depicted as the "Tree of Life (Proverbs 3.18)," a symbol representing the interconnectedness of all existence and the heavenly source of wisdom. Just as a tree provides nourishment and sustenance to all living beings, so too does the Torah offer spiritual nourishment to the soul, providing guidance and direction in navigating the complexities of life. We are told in **Deuteronomy 8.3** that "*...man does not live by bread alone but every Word that comes from the mouth of YaH.*" This principle that the bread of life pertains to the Torah was further made clear by Yeshua as He taught his disciples that "*the bread of Elohim is He who came down out of the heaven and gives life to the world.*" As the idiom "we are what eat" pertains to our physical health, so too does it apply to our spiritual well-being.

The purpose of Torah, as understood through the lens of Israel's inner eye, is to elevate humanity to higher levels of consciousness and spiritual awareness. By studying and observing the teachings of Torah, we are able to purify our souls, refine our character, and cultivate a deeper connection with YaH. Torah, as such, serves as a transformative tool, enabling us, as individuals and as a collective, to transcend our selfish desires and align ourselves with YaH's will.

Ultimately, the purpose of Torah, according to the Sages, is to bring about the Messianic people who incarnate the Torah and will orchestrate the Messianic redemption of humanity and the world. Through the study and observance of Torah, individuals can contribute to Tikkun Olam, the healing and repair of the world, and hasten the coming of the Messianic era. When perceived in its full scope, the Torah is not merely a set of rules to be followed but a living, breathing document that contains the wisdom of the ages and offers a path to spiritual enlightenment and redemption.

CHAPTER I
REFLECTING THE IMAGE AND LIKENESS OF ELOHIM

Genesis 1:26-27 - *"Then Elohim said, 'Let Us make mankind in Our image, in Our likeness, so that they may rule over the fish in the sea and the birds in the sky, over the livestock and all the wild animals, and over all the creatures that move along the ground.' So Elohim created mankind in His own image, in the image of Elohim He created them; male and female He created them."*

When we hear the phrase "the image and likeness of Elohim," we typically think in anthropomorphic terms relative to the Creator. And while modern man is in need of more material points of reference to capture abstract notions such as this, our earlier predecessors were masters of literary devices and used anthropomorphisms to capture the complex, and even mystical ideas that they were seeking to convey. We find this notion best explained by the 12th century Israelite philosopher Moshe ben Maimon, also known as Maimonides and the Rambam. In his masterpiece work entitled **The Guide for the Perplexed**[8]**,** the Rambam provides clarity regarding the Hebrew word used for image at Genesis 1. After showing the difference between the Hebrew word used for an actual appearance and form, toar/תֹּאַר, he goes on to state that *"[t]he term ẓelem/צֶלֶם...signifies the specific form, viz., that which constitutes the essence of a thing, whereby the thing is what it is; the reality of a thing in so far as it is that particular being. In man the "form" is that constituent which gives him human perception: and on account of this intellectual perception the term ẓelem is employed in the sentences "In the ẓelem of Elohim He created him" (Gen. 1. 27).*[9]

In the same chapter the Rambam continues to elaborate on this profound phrase from Genesis, bringing into focus the principle of likeness. "*Demut/דְּמוּת is derived from the verb damah, 'he is like.' This term likewise denotes agreement with regard to some abstract relation: comp. "I am like a pelican of the wilderness" (Ps. cii. 7); the author does not compare himself to the pelican in point of wings and feathers, but in point of sadness." Nor any tree in the garden of [Elohim] was like unto him in beauty" (Ezek. 8); the comparison refers to the idea of beauty."*[10] Here, the principle of likeness is relative to the dynamic of similitude and brings into focus the reality of the nature of humanity, in intent, being similar to the nature of its Creator.

Our major undertaking as humanity, is found in the letter of 1st John chapter 3 verses 1 and 2 where the beloved disciple writes, "*Beloved ones, now we are children of Elohim. And it has not yet been revealed what we shall be, but we know that when He is revealed,* ***we shall be like Him****, for we shall see Him as He is. And everyone having this expectation in Him cleanses himself, as He is clean.*"

As is apparent in both the Hebrew and Messianic Scriptures, the concept of humanity reflecting the image and likeness of Elohim is central to understanding our purpose and identity. From a rabbinic and Kabbalistic[11] perspective, this concept carries profound spiritual and metaphysical significance, highlighting humanity's unique role in creation.

From a rabbinic standpoint, these verses teach that in potentiality every human being, regardless of race, gender or creed, possesses inherent dignity and worth as they are created in the image of Elohim. It is humanity's purpose to discover and actualize this supreme reality. In consideration of this endeavor, we must be aware that the divine image is seen as encompassing qualities such as intellect, moral reasoning, the capacity for creativity and spiritual awareness, as well as conducting oneself in a righteous and holy manner. By reflecting these attributes, humanity fulfills its role as stewards of creation, tasked with caring for the Earth and its inhabitants in a manner that reflects the benevolent nature of our Creator.

In the Mishna[12], the foundational text of rabbinic ideology, there are several teachings that reflect the concept of humanity being created in the image and likeness of Elohim. While the Mishna itself does not explicitly quote verses from the Hebrew Scriptures, its teachings are deeply rooted in the biblical tradition and often draw upon biblical themes and concepts, providing its readers with insights from the sages about various passages and themes from Scripture. Here are some Mishnaic teachings that touch upon the image and likeness of Elohim:

1. **Mishnah Sanhedrin 4:5**:

"Therefore, Adam the first was created alone, to teach us that whoever destroys a single life, the Bible considers it as if he destroyed an entire world. And whoever saves a single life, the Bible considers it as if he saved an entire world."

This teaching emphasizes the sanctity and value of human life, reflecting the belief that each individual is created in the image and likeness of Elohim. Just as Adam, the first human with YaH consciousness, was created as a single individual, so too is each person seen as a unique and precious creation of YaH.

2. **Mishnah Avot 3:18**:

"Beloved is man, for he was created in the image [of Elohim]; it was an act of even greater love that it was made known to him that he was created in the image [of Elohim], as it is said: 'For in the image of Elohim He made man.'"

This teaching from Pirkei Avot[13] (Ethics of the Fathers) affirms the inherent dignity and value of humanity by emphasizing that each person is created in the image of Elohim. It highlights the special relationship between humanity and YaH, underscoring the love and care with which human beings are created by Elohim.

These Mishnaic teachings, while not quoting verses directly, reflect the profound theological concept of humanity's creation in the image and likeness of Elohim. They affirm the sanctity of human life, the inherent value of each individual, and the special relationship between humanity and YaH.

Kabbalistic teachings delve deeper into the metaphysical implications of humanity reflecting the image and likeness of Elohim. In Kabbalah, the divine image is not seen as a physical likeness but as a reflection of the spiritual attributes of the sefirot[14], the divine emanations through which YaH's energy flows into the world. Humanity's role is to align with these divine attributes, thereby becoming vessels for the presence of the Shekinah presence of Elohim in the material world.

The "Sefer Yetzirah" and the "Zohar" are two foundational texts from Kabbalah, or the Israelite hidden tradition of Torah interpretation. They contain teachings that delve into the nature of the image and likeness of Elohim from a Kabbalistic perspective. Much like the Mishnah, neither text explicitly quotes verses from the Hebrew Scriptures, they offer profound insights into the inner comprehension of humanity's relationship with YaH based on the principles and ideas of Scripture. The following are quotes from these texts regarding the image and likeness of Elohim:

From the Sefer Yetzirah:

1. **Sefer Yetzirah 1:7**:

"Ten Sefirot of Nothingness: Their measure is ten which have no end. A depth of beginning, a depth of end; a depth of good, a depth of evil; a depth of above, a depth of below; a depth of east, a depth of west; a depth of north, a depth of south. The singular Master, Elohim, faithful King, rules over all of them from His holy dwelling place until eternity of eternities."

This passage from the Sefer Yetzirah describes the Ten Sefirot, the divine emanations through which Elohim creates and sustains the universe. It emphasizes the unity and sovereignty of YaH, who governs all aspects of existence from Its transcendent realm. Humanity, as created beings, reflects the divine attributes inherent in these Sefirot, serving as vessels through which the Shekinah presence is manifested in the world.

From the Zohar:

2. **Zohar I:15a**:

"Man was created in the image of Elohim; He formed him in the likeness of His countenance, male and female He created them. This indicates that Adam, when he was created, had a spiritual appearance. As soon as he sinned, he dropped this form and assumed another form, which is ours."

In this passage from the Zohar, the text reflects on the creation of Adam and the significance of being made in the image and likeness of Elohim. It suggests that Adam originally possessed a spiritual form that mirrored the divine likeness, but this form was lost after he sinned. The Zohar explores the implications of humanity's fall from favor and the journey towards spiritual restoration and redemption.

These quotes from the Sefer Yetzirah and the Zohar offer glimpses into the Kabbalistic understanding of the image and likeness of Elohim. They convey the inner teachings regarding the divine emanations, the nature of humanity's relationship with YaH, and the spiritual journey towards unity with the Sovereign of the heavens and earth.

From a Messianic perspective, the image and likeness of Elohim are restored and renewed through the redemptive work of Yeshua as the Messiah. By following the teachings of Yeshua and being transformed by the indwelling of the Holy Spirit, we as disciples are empowered to reflect the image and likeness of Elohim more fully in our lives, embodying qualities such as love, compassion and righteousness.

Colossians 3:9-10 - *"Do not lie to each other, since you have put off the old man with his practices, and have put on the new one who is renewed in knowledge according to the likeness of Him who created him..."*

The concept of humanity reflecting the image and likeness of Elohim is a foundational principle in both the Hebrew and Messianic Scriptures. It is a principle that highlights humanity's inherent dignity and role as stewards of creation. It is a dynamic that underscores humanity's potential to be vessels for the Shekinah presence of YaH in the world. From a Messianic perspective, reflecting the image and likeness of Elohim speaks to the transformative power of the Messiah's redemptive work in restoring and renewing the imprint of the heavenly image within humanity.

As we expand upon the idea of humanity's purpose of reflecting the image and likeness of Elohim, let us now delve deeper into the concept of the heavenly imprint of **YaHuWaH**[15]. In the Hebrew language, the personal name of the Creator (Yod-Heh-Wah-Heh) represents the ineffable essence of Elohim, the Source from which all creation emanates. This Heavenly Imprint, inherent in every human soul, allows for us to clothe ourselves with the nature and essence of Elohim, aligning our very essence with the will of YaH and thereby come to reflect the middot[16], or the righteous and holy attributes of YaH[17] in our lives.

As a matter of fact, the Heavenly Imprint of YaH is not merely a static mark upon our souls, but a dynamic force that animates and enlivens our entire being. It is the very spark of life within us, the innermost essence that connects us to the transcendent realm and imbues us with the potential for spiritual greatness. Through the cultivation of awareness and alignment with this Heavenly Imprint, we can awaken to our true identity as reflections of YaH and fulfill our highest purpose on earth.

In Hebraic inner thought, or what again is known as Kabbalah, the Heavenly Imprint of YaH is associated with the sefirah, or sphere of Keter, the crown. Keter represents the highest aspect of heavenly consciousness attainable to humanity (James 1.12), and as we strive to embody the qualities of Keter—such as unity, harmony and transcendence—we become vessels for the primordial light of creation[18] to shine forth into the world. This process of self-transformation involves the purification of the ego, the refinement of character traits and the cultivation of virtues such as love, compassion and humility. I have already addressed this transformation when I referred to 1 John 3.1-2.

In further consideration of this self-transformation process, let us consider the following undertakings. In the Messianic tradition, the purification of the ego is understood as a fundamental aspect of spiritual transformation and alignment with the will of YaH. Messiah Yeshua taught extensively about the necessity of humility, selflessness and submission in the process of spiritual growth. One of the central teachings of Yeshua regarding the purification of the ego is found in Matthew 16:24-25, where he declares, *"If anyone would come after me, let him deny himself and take up his stake and follow me. For whoever would save his life will lose it, but whoever loses his life for my sake will find it."* This profound statement emphasizes the need to let go of the ego's desires and attachments in order to fully embrace the path of discipleship and heavenly service. This type of self-transformation leads to a life lived in accordance with the will of YaH, characterized by humility, love and selflessness.

The refinement of character traits, as discussed earlier in the context of middot, is a central aspect of the spiritual journey towards embodying the image and likeness of Elohim. Middot, righteous characteristics or ethical virtues, serve as guiding principles that shape our thoughts, words and actions, leading us towards greater alignment with YaH's attributes. Through intentional practice and cultivation of middot such as compassion, humility, patience and gratitude, we further undergo our process of inner transformation that enables us to transcend ego-driven desires and align ourselves with the will of YaH. As we refine our character traits, we become vessels for the expression of heaven's qualities in the world, bringing healing, harmony and wholeness to ourselves and others.

We complete the process of self-transformation when we are found in Yeshua and He in us. It is then that the embodiment of heaven's love and compassion is manifest within us and we find ourselves able to carry out the ultimate expression of bearing the image and likeness of Elohim. By following the teachings and actions of Yeshua, we are empowered to embody and exemplify the importance of cultivating virtues such as love, compassion and humility in our lives. As disciples of Yeshua, we are called to emulate our Master's example, allowing the Torah-based qualities of love, compassion and humility to shine forth in our thoughts, words and deeds. It is through the cultivation of these virtues that we truly reflect the image and likeness of Elohim, bringing light and healing to a world in need, fulfilling the greatest mystery spoken of in Scripture, as we are told by rabbi Sha'ul of Tarsus in his letter to the assembly at Colosse, "*...the secret which has been hidden from ages and from generations, but now has been revealed to His set-apart ones, to whom Elohim desired to make known what are the riches of the esteem of this secret among the gentiles:* ***which is Messiah in you****, the expectancy of esteem, whom we announce, warning every man and teaching every man in all wisdom, in order to present every man perfect in Messiah יהושע...*" *(Colossians 1.26-28).*

In light of our Messianic identity, it is imperative of us that we intimately come to know our responsibility to make the reality of the image and likeness of Elohim apparent on Earth; that we must come to know that the Heavenly Imprint of YaH encompasses the marriage of masculine and feminine energies within the heavenly unity. Balancing our nature is essential as relates to establishing the oneness that is to pervade all of creation. As the masculine and feminine principles are present in all things, functioning in harmony to establish the balance of nature, so too must we establish our nature by harnessing and mastering the masculine and feminine dynamics that are present within each of us. Just as Elohim is described in the Scriptures as encompassing both male and female principles—reflecting the complementary aspects of creative power and nurturing love—so too do we, as reflections of YaH, embody these dual aspects within ourselves and with one another. By embracing and integrating these masculine and feminine qualities, we achieve a state of balance and wholeness that allows for the fullest expression of our heavenly nature as individuals and as a collective.

The concept of the oneness of humanity found within the masculine and feminine principles is deeply rooted in the Messianic understanding of the union between Messiah Yeshua and his disciples. As we've previously mentioned, in Ephesians 5:31-32, Rabbi Sha'ul draws upon the imagery of marriage to illustrate the profound mystery of the relationship between Yeshua and his bride, the entire household of faith. Shaul quotes from Genesis 2:24, stating, *"For this reason a man will leave his father and mother and be united to his wife, and the two will become one flesh."* He then declares, *"This is a profound mystery—but I am talking about Messiah and the assembly."*

Here, Shaul reveals that the union between husband and wife serves as a symbol of the deeper spiritual reality of the oneness between Yeshua and his disciples; the Messiah as Head and the Body of Messiah. Just as a husband and wife become one flesh in marriage, so too does Yeshua and his disciples become spiritually united through study and faithful obedience. This spiritual oneness transcends individual identities and distinctions, creating a new entity—the body of Messiah—that is united in purpose, destiny, desire and heavenly love.

Furthermore, Ephesians 5:31-32 emphasizes the sacrificial love, selflessness and submission that characterize the union between Yeshua and his bride. Just as Yeshua gave himself up for the assembly, so too are disciples called to love one another sacrificially (John 15.13), seeking the good of others above themselves. This mutual love and unity among disciples serves as an authentic witness to the world of the transformative power of the Good News and the reality of YaH's kingdom on earth.

In essence, Ephesians 5:31-32 underscores the profound truth of the oneness of humanity in Messiah Yeshua. Through our faithfulness to him, we are united with Yeshua and with one another, forming a spiritual bond that transcends all earthly divisions and distinctions. This unity in Messiah reflects the image and likeness of Elohim, manifesting the heavenly love, compassion and humility that righteously characterizes the Kingdom of Heaven.

Ultimately, when we are able to attain and maintain the purification of our ego, the refinement of our character traits and the cultivation of righteous virtues, it is then that the recognition and realization of the Heavenly Imprint of YaH within ourselves will become key to fulfilling our highest purpose as human beings. It is through this heavenly connection that we are then empowered to co-create with YaH, to participate in the ongoing process of cosmic evolution and to bring forth the Kingdom of Heaven on Earth. As we awaken to the truth of our heavenly heritage and align ourselves with the will of YaH, we become agents of the primordial light and eternal love of YaH, illuminating the world with the radiance of our true selves.

Adam, the Prototype of Humanity's Heavenly Identity

Transitioning from the section on the Heavenly Imprint to the principle of Adam as the Prototype, we move from the abstract concept of humanity's heavenly essence to the practical manifestation of this truth for humanity taking principles from the account of Adam, the primordial archetype of humanity. Just as every human soul carries the imprint of Heaven, so too does Adam serve as the paradigmatic expression of this Heavenly Identity. This principle is vividly illustrated in the vision of the Tabernacle that Moses was shown on the mountain, a vision that served as a blueprint for the earthly sanctuary. In Exodus 25:9, YaH instructs Moses, "*According to all that I show you*, *take heed*, *the pattern of the tabernacle and the pattern of all its furnishings*, *you shall make it exactly according to the pattern*." This revelation to Moses underscores the idea that the earthly realm is a reflection of the heavenly reality, and how Adam, as the prototype of humanity, embodies this heavenly pattern in his very being.

Oral tradition further explains the significance of this vision of the Tabernacle which serves as a reflection of Adam's Heavenly Identity. In Midrash Tanchuma (Pekudei 4), it is taught that the Mishkan, or Tabernacle, represents the microcosm of creation with its various components corresponding to different aspects of the cosmos. The Tabernacle is seen as a symbolic representation of the Shekinah Presence dwelling among humanity, mirroring the intimate relationship between YaH and Adam in the Garden of Eden. Similarly, in the Zohar (Parashat Terumah[19]), the Tabernacle is described as a reflection of the supernal realms, with its construction and arrangement mirroring the divine order of creation. This mystical interpretation emphasizes the interconnectedness of the earthly and heavenly realms, and the central role of Adam as the bridge between them.

In unraveling the mysteries of Heavenly Identity through the example of the vision of the Tabernacle, we come to understand that Adam is not merely a historical figure, but a timeless archetype that embodies the heavenly blueprint for humanity. Just as the Tabernacle was meticulously constructed according to the heavenly pattern revealed to Moses, so too are we called to align ourselves with the divine image and likeness imprinted upon us. As we explore the depths of Adam's prototype, we discover the profound truth that our Heavenly Identity is not something to be attained, but something to be remembered and reclaimed—a sacred inheritance that has been entrusted to us from the beginning of creation.

Building upon the similarities between Adam as the prototype in Genesis 1 and the Tabernacle in Exodus 25.9, we find further confirmation of this concept in both Scripture and Israel's oral tradition from Chazal (Sages of Israel)[20]. In Genesis 1:27-28 Adam is depicted as the pinnacle of creation, created in the image and likeness of Elohim and given the heavenly mandate to rule over the earth. This echoes the purpose of the Tabernacle, which serves as a dwelling place for the Shekinah Presence on earth, reflecting the heavenly order and fulfilling the divine purpose of creation.

The sages of Israel further expound upon the similarities between Adam and the Tabernacle in their teachings. In Midrash Rabbah (Bereishit Rabbah 8:5), it is taught that just as Adam was clothed in garments of light before his sin, so too was the Tabernacle adorned with garments of esteem and beauty. This parallel underscores the idea that both Adam and the Tabernacle represent manifestations of heavenly splendor and perfection (Urim and Tummim), reflecting the heavenly prototype in their earthly form. Similarly, in Midrash Tanhuma (Pekudei 3), it is said that just as Adam was created on the sixth day, so too was the Tabernacle assembled on the sixth day of the consecration process. This connection emphasizes the sacred significance of the Tabernacle as a symbol of humanity's restored heavenly nature.

Moreover, the Mishnah in Avot (5:1) teaches that "the world was created with relationship with YaH, mirroring the celestial harmony and unity of the original creation with ten utterances." This rabbinic teaching highlights the idea that creation itself is a reflection of divine speech, with each utterance representing a different aspect of the cosmic order. In this context, Adam as the prototype of humanity and the Tabernacle as the microcosm of creation, both embody the divine utterances in their form and function serving as tangible expressions of the heavenly will and sovereign purpose of YaH.

In reflection, the similarities between Adam in Genesis 1.26 and the Tabernacle in Exodus 29.5 underscore the profound connection between humanity and the Shekinah Presence of YaH on earth. Both Adam and the Tabernacle represent manifestations of the heavenly prototype, reflecting the heavenly image and sovereign purpose in their earthly form. Through Scripture and oral tradition from Chazal, we gain insight into the sacred significance of both Adam and the Tabernacle as symbols of heavenly revelation and prophetic redemption, inviting us to explore the depths of our Heavenly Identity and our intimate relationship with YaH.

As we continue to delve deep into the process of rediscovering our true nature and reclaiming the image and likeness of Elohim within us, let us now consider what our journey entails. At its core, this journey is about reconnecting with the divine nature that lies dormant within each of us, obscured by layers of conditioning, egoic patterns, and worldly distractions. It is a journey of awakening to the reality of who we truly are—divine beings created in the image and likeness of Elohim.

To rediscover our true nature is to peel back layers of illusion and falsehood that have veiled our perception of reality. It requires a willingness to confront the narratives of limitation and separation that have been ingrained in us from an early age, and to question the validity of the beliefs and identities that we have adopted. Perhaps most importantly, it requires us to unlearn the years of false doctrines, misinformation and misperceptions that have yielded states of cognitive dissonance that dominate many of our mind states. As we embark on this journey of self-discovery, we are invited to explore the depths of our innermost being, to listen to the whispers of our soul, and to align ourselves with the divine presence that dwells within.

Reclaiming the image of Elohim is a process of cultural reconnaissance and spiritual restoration, of remembering and re-embodying the qualities of YaH identified in the Torah that actually are our birthright. It is a journey of transformation and metamorphosis, as we shed the layers of falsehood and limitation and step into the fullness of our heavenly potential. In reclaiming the image and likeness of Elohim, we reclaim our power, our purpose, and our inherent dignity as beloved children of the Most High. We recognize that we are co-creators with YaH, endowed with the capacity to bring forth beauty, goodness and abundance in the world.

As we rediscover our true nature and reclaim the reflection of Elohim within us, we become agents of healing and transformation in the world; or what we've already identified as Tikkun Olam. When the image and likeness is manifest within us, we embody the qualities of love, compassion and wisdom that are the hallmarks of the beneficent One. When we embody the qualities of love, compassion and wisdom, we shine forth as beacons of light in a world that is often shrouded in darkness. Through our words and actions, we inspire others to awaken to their own divine nature and, together, we co-create a world that reflects the beauty and goodness of YaH.

Our journey of rediscovering our true nature and reclaiming the reflection of Elohim is the journey of a lifetime—a journey of self-discovery, self-empowerment and self-realization. Higher than any exploration up a mountain or into space, deeper than any expedition to the bottom of the ocean, our journey of rediscover is a journey that leads us back to the Source of all life, to the heart of YaH, and to the realization that we are one with all that is. May we embrace this journey with open hearts and open minds, trusting in the guidance of the Most High as we awaken to the truth of who we are at our core and why we are here in truth, as we return to the primordial and sovereign order of YaH when the words, "*let there be light*," was said.

PARABLE OF THE PRESENCE OF CONCEALED LIGHT

In a kingdom far beyond the realms of ordinary sight there existed a magnificent palace made entirely of radiant light. This palace was the abode of YaH, the King of Light, whose brilliance illuminated the entire kingdom, filling it with warmth, love and wisdom. The subjects of this kingdom lived in harmony, guided by the principles of the King who taught them the ways of justice, compassion and humility.

However, not far from this luminous kingdom lay a vast, shadowy forest known as the Forest of Kelipot. The kelipot were dark, thorny shells that captured and held captive the sparks of the King's light, obscuring their glow and trapping them within layers of seemingly impenetrable darkness. The forest was a place of ignorance, fear and evil, where creatures lurked in the shadows, spreading despair and chaos. The light within the kelipot was hidden, and few believed that anything good could come from such a place.

One day, a young and courageous prince from the palace named Or decided to venture into the Forest of Kelipot. He had heard tales of the hidden sparks of light and was determined to uncover them and restore their brilliance. Armed with the teachings of the King and a heart full of love and faith, Or embarked on his journey into the darkness.

As Or navigated the treacherous forest, he encountered many obstacles. The kelipot were formidable, their shells thick and seemingly unbreakable. The creatures of the forest whispered words of doubt and fear, trying to dissuade him from his mission. But Or remembered the King's teachings and remained steadfast. He used the light of his wisdom to see through the illusions of the forest and the warmth of his love to melt the barriers of the kelipot.

With each kelipah he encountered, Or would patiently work to pierce through its darkness. He would speak words of truth and kindness, and as he did the kelipah would begin to crack. Slowly but surely, the hidden spark within would start to shine, its light growing brighter and brighter until it burst forth, illuminating the forest around it.

As Or continued his journey, the once dark and foreboding forest began to transform. The light from the freed sparks spread, connecting with other hidden lights and creating a network of illumination that dispelled the shadows. The creatures of the forest, once agents of darkness, were themselves touched by the light and began to change. They became allies in Or's quest, helping him to find and free more hidden sparks.

News of Or's success reached the palace, and the King of Light was overjoyed. He proclaimed that Or's journey was a testament to the power of knowledge and love to overcome ignorance and evil. The King declared that every subject of the kingdom had the potential to be a bearer of light, capable of piercing through the darkness of the kelipot and revealing the hidden brilliance within.

In time, the entire forest was transformed into a place of beauty and light, its once dark and thorny kelipot now replaced with radiant beacons of hope and wisdom. The kingdom flourished as never before, with the light of the hidden sparks illuminating every corner, banishing ignorance and fear.

This parable of the Hidden Light teaches us that within every layer of darkness and ignorance, there lies a hidden spark of divine light waiting to be revealed. Through perseverance, wisdom and love, we can pierce through the kelipot, dispelling the shadows and bringing forth the brilliance of knowledge, love and goodness. Just as Or's journey transformed the Forest of Kelipot, so too can our efforts to embody the principles of the King of Light bring about a world filled with understanding, compassion and divine radiance.

Interestingly, in Kabbalah, the concept of kelipot[21] (singular: klippah) refers to the husks or shells that conceal our primordial nature of the divine light and energy within creation. These kelipot are seen as veils that obscure the Shekinah Presence of YaH within us, creating a barrier between the material world and the spiritual realm. According to Kabbalistic teachings, the universe is permeated with heavenly energy, but this energy is often captured, obscured or distorted by the presence of kelipot.

The term "kelipot" originates from the metaphor of a shell or husk that surrounds and protects a fruit or seed. In the Kabbalistic tradition, the kelipot are understood as spiritual impediments that obstruct the flow of divine light into the world. They represent the forces of negativity, impurity and spiritual stagnation that hinder the soul's ascent towards enlightenment and unity with YaH.

However, despite their negative connotations, the kelipot also serve a purpose within the cosmic order. In the Kabbalistic worldview, the kelipot are not inherently evil or malevolent, rather they represent the potential for spiritual growth and transformation. The process of overcoming the kelipot is seen as essential for the soul's evolution and refinement, as it involves confronting and transcending the obstacles that stand in the way of the connection between Heaven and Earth, Spirit and Flesh.

From a Kabbalistic perspective, the kelipot encapsulate the primordial light and intelligent energy that animates our souls and bodies. This divine energy is said to be trapped within the kelipot, awaiting liberation and redemption. Through spiritual practices such as prayer, meditation, acts of kindness, repentance and the fulfillment of the commandments, we can gradually peel away the layers of kelipot that obscure our heavenly nature, allowing the primordial light to shine forth and illuminate our consciousness.

The Scriptures provide us a tale about our body's journey with the soul when connected with YaH. This process is one of our liberation from the kelipot and reunification with YaH. By transcending the limitations of the material world and purifying our soul from the influence of the kelipot, we are able to attain a state of unity with YaH and experience the fullness of our spiritual potential. In this way, the concept of kelipot in Kabbalah serves as a reminder of the inherent heavenly nature within each of our souls and the transformative power of spiritual awakening. Scriptural references to the concept of kelipot can be found in various passages that speak of darkness, impurity and spiritual obstruction. For example, in Isaiah 5:20, it is written, *"Woe to those who call evil good and good evil, who put darkness for light and light for darkness."* This verse highlights the inversion of truth and goodness caused by the influence of kelipot, which distort perception and lead to moral confusion. It is clear to see that our present society has allowed for this obfuscation of reality to take hold of the masses, inverting the eternal principles of life which have held creation together in harmony for eons into counterproductive, relative notions.

The Zohar, a foundational text of Kabbalah, offers extensive teachings on the nature of kelipot and their role in the order of creation. In Parashat Bereshit (Zohar I:15a), it is said that before the creation of the world, there existed a realm of darkness and chaos, known as Tohu (chaos) and Bohu (emptiness). From this primordial state, YaH emanated a ray of light that shattered the darkness, giving rise to the creation of the universe. However, remnants of this primordial darkness remained, forming the Kelipot that continue to obscure the divine light within creation.

The Mishnah also contains teachings that touch upon the concept of kelipot, albeit indirectly. In Pirkei Avot (1:7), it is stated, *"Nittai the Arbelite used to say: keep a distance from an evil neighbor, do not become attached to the wicked, and do not abandon faith in [divine] retribution."* Nittai the Arbelite's teaching emphasizes the importance of maintaining moral integrity by avoiding negative influences which can lead to the ensnaring forces of the kelipot. Keeping a distance from an evil neighbor and not becoming attached to the wicked are admonitions to steer clear of corrupting influences that often lead one astray and into the web of kelipot. The exhortation to not abandon faith while experiencing wrath in moments of divine retribution underscores the belief in ultimate justice and accountability, reinforcing the importance of righteous living and trust in the Torah's governance.

The concept of kelipot further encapsulates the idea of spiritual obstruction and impurity that obscures the primordial light within creation. Drawing upon scriptural references, the Zohar, and the teachings of the Mishnah, those in pursuit of returning to their primordial nature delve into the mechanics of kelipot and their role in the cosmic order, seeking to overcome their influence and liberate the heavenly sparks of light trapped within. Through spiritual practice, ethical living and mystical contemplation, practitioners of Torah strive to pierce through the veils of kelipot and reveal the primordial light and intelligent energy that animates our souls and bodies.

Lastly, we see that the concept of kelipot offers us a profound lens through which we are able to understand the challenges of darkness that pervade humanity and the world today. In our day, we witness numerous manifestations of spiritual obstruction and impurity that obscure the primordial light within creation, echoing the primordial chaos of Tohu and Bohu. From global conflicts and environmental degradation to social injustices and moral decay, the darkness of humanity abounds in various forms, reflecting the residual influences of kelipot that continue to cast shadows upon our world. Yet and still, there is hope.

One striking example of the impact of kelipot on humanity today can be seen in the prevalence of violence and conflict around the world. Wars, terrorism, and armed conflicts result in immense suffering and loss of life, perpetuating cycles of hatred and division that deepen the veil of darkness over the collective consciousness. The root causes of these conflicts often lie in greed, power struggles and the dehumanization of others—a reflection of the ego-driven impulses that fuel the kelipot and perpetuate spiritual obstruction.

Furthermore, environmental degradation and ecological crises serve as stark reminders of the consequences of humanity's disconnection from the heavenly order of creation. Pollution, deforestation, and climate change threaten the delicate balance of ecosystems and jeopardize the well-being of future generations. These crises stem from a lack of holistic awareness of and reverence for the sacredness of the earth. These glaring deficiencies stem from systemic failures to recognize our interconnectedness with all living beings—a distortion of perception that aligns with the influence of the kelipot.

In addition to external events, the darkness of humanity is also evident in the prevalence of perversity, moral decay and ethical lapses that characterize modern society. Corruption, greed and moral relativism erode the foundations of trust, integrity and compassion that are essential for a thriving and harmonious community. The pursuit of material wealth and worldly pleasures often takes precedence over spiritual values and ethical principles, leading to a pervasive sense of spiritual emptiness and alienation—a reflection of the spiritual void left by the influence of kelipot.

In confronting the darkness of humanity today, it is essential to recognize the role of the kelipot and to actively work towards overcoming their influence through spiritual practice, ethical living and compassionate action. By cultivating awareness, empathy and a sense of interconnectedness with all of creation, we can begin to pierce through the veils of darkness and reveal the heavenly light of Torah that resides within each and every one of us. Through acts of kindness, justice and love, we can become agents of transformation and healing, contributing to the gradual liberation of the divine sparks of light trapped within the kelipot and the realization of a world illuminated by the radiance of the Shekinah Presence of YaH on Earth.

As we draw to a close with Chapter 1, it is essential to reflect on the profound parallels between Genesis 1 and the first chapter of the Witness of John, particularly in their exploration of the themes of light and darkness. In Genesis 1, we witness the divine act of creation, where Elohim speaks light into existence, dispelling the primordial darkness and bringing order to the formless void. This primordial light serves as a symbol of divine revelation, truth and goodness, illuminating the path towards divine purpose and fulfillment.

Similarly, in the Witness of John we encounter the profound declaration that "*In the beginning was the Word, and the Word was with Elohim, and the Word was Elohim. He was in the beginning with Elohim. All things were made through him, and without him was not anything made that was made. In him was life, and the life was the light of men. The light shines in the darkness, and the darkness has not overcome it*" (John 1:1-5). Here, Yeshua the Messiah is portrayed as the pre-incarnate Word, or Torah made flesh; the embodiment of the primordial light that shines in the darkness, offering hope, redemption and salvation to humanity.

In this role, Yeshua is perceived as the Master Workman, bringing both form and order to the formlessness and void that once covered the face of the Earth. We find this dynamic expressed in Proverbs, where King Solomon gives a graphic description of wisdom in anthropomorphic terms carrying out its purpose according to the Will of YaH. Revealing the Torah as the hands through which all of creation was brought forth, Solomon wrote,

"YaH possessed me, the beginning of His way, as the first of His works of old. I was set up ages ago, at the first, before the earth ever was...Then I was beside Him, a master workman, and I was His delight, day by day Rejoicing before Him all the time, rejoicing in the world, His earth; And my delights were with the sons of men (Proverbs 8.22-23, 30-31).

In both Genesis 1 and John 1, we, as agents of transformation and a kingdom of priests are called to be light in the midst of darkness; to embody the divine qualities of truth, love and righteousness that dispel ignorance, hatred and sin. Just as YaH separated light from darkness in the act of creation, so too are we called to be set apart from the darkness of the world, to live lives of holiness and purity that reflect the heavenly image and likeness imprinted upon us. As disciples of Yeshua, we are called to emulate his example, to walk in the light of his teachings, and to be beacons of hope and healing in a world that is often shrouded in darkness by the kelipot.

This principle is also explained in Ephesians 5:8-17, where we are reminded of our identity as children of light: "*For at one time you were darkness, but now you are light in YaH. Walk as children of light - for the fruit of the Spirit is in all goodness, and righteousness and truth, proving what is well-pleasing to the Master. And have no fellowship with the fruitless works of darkness, but rather reprove them. For it is a shame even to speak of what is done by them in secret. But all matters being reproved are manifested by the light, for whatever is manifested is light. That is why He says, 'Wake up, you who sleep, and arise from the dead, and Messiah shall shine on you.' See then that you walk exactly, not as unwise, but as wise, redeeming the time, because the days are wicked. So then do not be foolish, but understand what the desire of YaH is."*

This passage underscores the transformative power of the Good News[22], which has liberated us from the bondage of sin, death and darkness and brought us into the light of YaH's love and favor. As children of light, we are called to live lives of righteousness and holiness, to shine forth as witnesses to the truth of the Good News, and to bring esteem to YaH in all that we do.

As we prepare to transition to the next chapter, let us again reflect on the profound nexus of truths revealed in Genesis 1, John 1 and Ephesians 5, boldly accepting and embracing our identity as bearers of the primordial light, called to illuminate the world with the radiance of YaH's love and truth. May we walk in the light of Yeshua's teachings, which illuminate and bring to life the Torah, instructing us to live lives of integrity, compassion and humility. And may our lives serve as a testament to the transformative power of the Good News to dispel darkness and bring forth the primordial Light of the Kingdom of Heaven on Earth as the Messianic Kingdom of Priests.

CHAPTER II
MASTERY OF SELF AND CREATION

In Genesis 1:28, we encounter another heavenly mandate given to humanity: "*And Elohim blessed them. And Elohim said to them, 'Be fruitful and multiply and fill the earth and subdue it.* ***Rule over the fish in the sea and the birds in the sky and over every living creature that moves on the ground***.'" This verse not only captures the absolute sovereignty of YaH, it also establishes the heavenly commission bestowed upon humanity to exercise rulership over creation. As the reflection of YaH on Earth, it is the role of humanity, led by the national priesthood of Israel, to establish a harmonic existence for all of creation in fulfillment of the prophetic pledge from Deuteronomy 6.4 that the people of the covenant declare twice daily with the words, "*hear O Israel, YaH is our Elohim, YaH is One.*" To understand the depth and significance of this mandate, we turn to both scripture and references from the oral tradition that illuminate the principles of sovereignty and rulership in the sovereign order of creation.

Scriptural references abound regarding the sovereignty of YaH and humanity's role in exercising rulership on earth. In Psalm 8:4-8, it is written, "*What is man that You remember him? And the son of man that You visit him? Yet You have made him a little less than Elohim and have crowned him with esteem and splendor.* ***You have given him dominion over the works of your hands; you have put all things under his feet, all sheep and oxen, and also the beasts of the field, the birds of the heavens, and the fish of the sea, whatever passes along the paths of the seas***." This passage underscores humanity's heavenly ordained authority to both govern and steward the earth, a reflection of the sovereignty of YaH manifested in the created order.

To illustrate this principle idiomatically, rabbinic teachings offer insights into the principles of rulership and sovereignty in the cosmic order. In Pirkei Avot (4:1), it is written, *"Who is strong? One who overpowers his inclinations, as it is said: 'Better is the one who is slow to anger than the mighty, and one who rules his spirit than one who captures a city (Proverbs 16.32).'"* This Mishnaic teaching emphasizes the importance of self-mastery and moral integrity in exercising rulership and authority. By aligning oneself with the will of YaH and governing one's thoughts, words and actions in accordance with the principles of the Torah, one becomes a true ruler over self and creation in principle, reflecting the sovereignty of YaH in Spirit and Truth.

Additionally, the Laws of Correspondence[23] and the Equivalence of Form[24] teach us that humanity's rulership on earth is intimately connected to its alignment with the sovereign will and heavenly attributes of YaH. Just as YaH reigns supreme in the heavens, so too are humans called to rule in YaH's place on earth, embodying the supernal qualities of wisdom, justice and love. Through the Law of Correspondence, humans are tasked with mirroring the heavenly order in their governance of the earth, ensuring conditions that lead to the manifestation of harmony, balance and the proliferation of life for all of creation.

The Law of Correspondence, also known as the principle of "as above, so below," is an essential element of the truth that makes up Universal Law. Universal Law is the order of fundamental reality that establishes the basis for existence, and ultimately, balance and accord in perpetuity. This particular law demonstrates that there is a correspondence between the macrocosm (the larger universe) and the microcosm (the individual), such as that the patterns, structures and dynamics found in the higher realms are able to be reflected in the lower realms. In the context of Torah and the mysteries of Israelite consciousness, the Law of Correspondence emphasizes the interconnectedness of the spiritual and material worlds, as well as the idea that earthly phenomena mirrors heavenly principles and realities. This dynamic we find alluded to by Yeshua when he stated, "*[YaH's] will be done, [YaH's] kingdom come on Earth as it is in Heaven*" (Matthew 6.10); and when he says, "*If you do not believe when I spoke to you about earthly matters, how are you going to believe when I speak to you about the heavenly matters*?" (John 3.12).

Scriptural references that support the Law of Correspondence can be found throughout the Torah and other Hebrew texts. For example, in Genesis 19.24, it is written, "And יהוה rained sulphur and fire on Seḏom and Amorah, from יהוה out of the heavens." This verse demonstrates the potential power derived from the nexus between heaven and earth when the presence of YaH is manifest above and below. This manifestation is achieved through the alignment of the will of the children of Light with that of the sovereign will of the Father of lights. So this is reflected in the verse, *"Deep calls to deep at the sound of Your waterfalls; all Your waves and breakers passed over me" (Psalm 42.7).* In this presents the call and response dynamic in fulfillment of the word in the heart of the soul responding to the Word from the mouth of YaH. And so we read this principle fulfilled in flesh as shown in Revelation 19.9, *"Write, 'Blessed are those who have been called to the marriage supper of the Lamb!' And he said to me, "These are the true words of Elohim."*

With the intent of awakening the Word within, it is every disciple's responsibility to undergo the transformative work that the Torah instructs for them to complete. For it is when self-mastery is achieved, then the soul that has attained a state of consciousness that causes them to bear the image of the likeness of YaH. This is how the Law of Correspondence works in our lives; bearing the image here below on Earth of the pattern established above in Heaven.

Pirkei Avot (3:17) also teaches the Law of Correspondence when it states, "*Reflect upon three things and you will not come to the hands of transgression: Know from where you came, where you are going, and before whom you are destined to give an account and reckoning.*" Underscoring the importance of introspection and self-awareness, this rabbinic teaching emphasizes the importance of recognizing the heavenly imprint within oneself and aligning one's thoughts, words and actions with heavenly purpose.

The Law of Equivalence of Form, on the other hand, brings to light the idea that spiritual growth and transformation require one to intentionally align oneself with the attributes and qualities (מִדּוֹת/middot) of YaH. In Kabbalistic teachings, this concept is often related to the dynamics of "Tikkun Olam," or the repair of the age, which involves rectifying the imbalance and disharmony caused by human thought forms and actions through the cultivation of righteousness and oneness.

Scriptural references that support the Law of Equivalence of Form include passages that speak to the importance of ethical conduct and moral integrity. For example, in Micah 6:8 it is written, "*He has shown you, O man, what is good. And what does YaH require of you? To act justly and to love mercy and to walk humbly with your Elohim.*" This verse highlights the connection between ethical behavior and our communion with heaven, suggesting that living in accordance with heavenly principles brings one closer to Elohim and given the number of souls aligned with the Torah, the stronger the Shekinah presence of YaH "ill be on earth.

Also from Pirkei Avot (2:1) we find this teaching, "*Rabban Gamliel, the son of Rabbi Judah the Prince, said: Great is Torah, for it gives life to those who practice it in this world and in the World to Come.*" This Mishnaic teaching establishes the transformative power of Torah study and observance in shaping one's character and aligning one's soul with heavenly truth. It also illuminates the result of the harmonic resonance between the soul and the Torah. 's the Word resonates at a ra'e that allows it to transcend time and space, so does the soul which through the Law of Equivalence of Form elevates its vibration. This feat is done by following the instructions of the Word, which in essence guides the soul to become the living manifestation of the Word. This we read in the words of Isaiah when he writes, "*Grass shall wither, the flower shall fade, but the Word of our Elohim stands forever.*"

In Deuteronomy 30.14, we see best see The Law of Correspondence and the Law of Equivalence of Form at work in the Torah. Exorting Israel to always choose life and to love YaH, Moses reminds them that "*the Word is very near you, in your mouth and in your heart – to do it.*" Herein lies the foundational principle in the Torah and the Israelite inner tradition that highlight the interconnectedness between the spiritual and material realms, and the importance of aligning oneself with heavenly principles and attributes. Through study, meditation, prayer and faithfulness, individuals can deepen their understanding of these laws and strive to live in harmony with the will of YaH.

In light of what we have just covered, we can see more fully how Genesis 1:28 presents humanity with the sacred mandate to establish rulership, reflecting the sovereignty of YaH and exercising dominion with wisdom and righteousness throughout creation. Through scriptural and Mishnaic references, we gain a deeper context with wider insight into the principles of the sovereignty and rulership of YaH in the cosmic order, as well as the Law of Correspondence and Equivalence of Form that governs humanity's relationship with YaH. As we embark on the journey of establishing rulership throughout creation, may we do so with humility, integrity and reverence for the sacred trust bestowed upon us by the King of kings and the Master of masters. Amein.

On our journey towards manifesting the image and likeness of Elohim, self-mastery emerges as a crucial aspect. Self-mastery is the art of controlling one's desires, emotions and actions in alignment with the wisdom of the Torah. It is the deliberate effort to align our inner world with the will of YaH, ensuring that our thoughts and behaviors reflect His holiness and righteousness.

As we delve into the Scriptures, the story of Cain and Abel in Genesis 4 stands out vividly. When Cain's offering was rejected, he became angry and dejected. Intellectually disarmed by his emotions, Cain's anger inflamed his gut, causing his lower vibrations to resonate throughout his being, invoking his murderous spirit. To provide him a way out, YaH addressed Cain directly to his conscience, saying, "*Why are you angry, and why has your countenance fallen? If you do well, will you not be accepted? And if you do not do well, sin is crouching at the door. Its desire is contrary to you, but you must master it*" (Genesis 4:6-7). As we know the rest of the tale, this passage is a profound illustration of the struggle against sin and the call to self-mastery. YaH's words to Cain are a reminder that we all have the potential to overcome sin, but it requires vigilance and control, or as Messiah Yeshua says, "*to watch and pray*" (Matthew 26.41).

Focusing on the purpose and reflecting on the words of 1 John 3:1-11, the call to self-mastery becomes even clearer. The beloved disciple John writes, "*See what great love the Father has lavished on us, that we should be called children of Elohim! And that is what we are! The reason the world does not know us is that it did not know him. Dear friends, now we are children of Elohim, and what we will be has not yet been made known.* ***But we know that when Messiah appears, we shall be like him, for we shall see him as he is. All who have this hope in him purify themselves, just as he is pure***" (1 John 3:1-3). This purification is the work initiated and maintained to manifest self-mastery which requires us to make a conscious effort to align our lives with the purity and holiness of the teachings and life of Yeshua.

John further emphasizes the victory over sin through the transformative power of YaH's love: "*No one who lives in him keeps on sinning. No one who continues to sin has either seen him or known him. Dear children, do not let anyone lead you astray. The one who does what is right is righteous, just as he is righteous. The one who does what is sinful is of the devil, because the devil has been sinning from the beginning. The reason the Son of Elohim appeared was to destroy the devil's work. No one who is born of Elohim will continue to sin, because Elohim's seed remains in them; they cannot go on sinning, because they have been born of Elohim. This is how we know who the children of Elohim are and who the children of the devil are: Anyone who does not do what is right is not Elohim's child, nor is anyone who does not love their brother and sister*" (1 John 3:6-10).

Self-mastery involves a deep, inner transformation where we actively work to purify ourselves from sinful desires. It requires us to cultivate virtues such as patience, humility and love. As we strive for self-mastery, we become more like Yeshua, embodying the divine principles he lived by.

We are told of the exact steps to take on this journey by the disciple Shim'on Kepha, also known as Simon Peter. At 2 Kepha 1.5-9, a challenge is issued by Kepha for the body of Messiah to increase its comprehensive fruitfulness. To fulfill this, Kepha explains the characteristics needed to become the reflection of the Son; "*...for this reason do your utmost to add to your faithfulness uprightness, to uprightness knowledge, to knowledge self-control, to self-control endurance, to endurance reverence, to reverence brotherly affection, and to brotherly affection love. For if these are in you and increase, they cause you to be neither inactive nor without fruit in the knowledge of our Master* יהושע *Messiah.*"

This journey of self-mastery is not only a personal endeavor but also a collective responsibility. As we support and encourage one another in our pursuit of righteousness, we move in the Spirit of the Torah knowing that the result of having a collective consciousness that informs us of our vision and purpose allows for the Shekinah to appear through our collective projection of light.

With this calling, the challenge of self-mastery is ever-present, but with the guidance of the Torah and the example of Yeshua, we are well equipped to overcome as Rabbi Sha'ul informed in Romans 8.37, *"we are more than overcomers through Him who loved us."* As we grow in self-mastery, we reflect more of Elohim's image, fulfilling our highest purpose and contributing to the establishment of His sovereign Kingdom on earth. Let it be known, the pursuit of self-mastery is a testament to our commitment to live as children of light, overcoming darkness and sin through the power of YaH's love and truth to reign over all the Earth as the children of Elohim.

Understanding the Mandate of Sovereignty

As we transition into the exploration of the principle of sovereignty in Scripture, it is imperative to begin with the foundational narrative of Genesis 1.1, where the sovereignty of YaH, as Creator, is established on the first day of creation. With this divine act of creation, YaH exercises absolute authority and power, bringing forth the heavens, the earth, the sea and all living creatures into existence with and by the power of the Word. This narrative serves as the cornerstone of the biblical axiom of sovereignty, emphasizing the supreme authority of YaH over all creation.

To assist with our comprehension of the matter of divine sovereignty, let us take a look at principles and concepts from political science which will shed light on the nature of the Kingdom of Heaven as a theocratic entity on Earth. Political science as a practice examines the structures, processes and dynamics of governance, providing insights into how power is exercised, legitimacy is conferred and authority is upheld within human societies. As a discipline, political science is intent on helping humans establish self-governance for the betterment of the world. When applied to the Kingdom of Heaven, these principles offer a framework for understanding how Heaven's sovereignty is manifested and administered in the earthly realm.

As I mentioned in the Kingdom Within, one key concept from political science that resonates with the theocratic nature of the Kingdom of Heaven is the idea of divine right monarchy[25]. In this political theory, monarchs derive their authority directly from "Elohim," and their rule is considered to be divinely ordained. Similarly, in the Kingdom of Heaven, the sovereignty of YaH is absolute and unassailable, and all earthly authority ultimately derives its legitimacy from the Elohim of Abraham, Isaac and Jacob. This principle underscores the divine origin of authority and the hierarchical order of the Kingdom, where YaH reigns supreme as the ultimate sovereign.

Moreover, the concept of theocracy, or rule by divine law, is central to understanding the governance structure of the Kingdom of Heaven. In a theocratic system, divine principles and commandments serve as the foundation of law and governance, guiding the actions and decisions of rulers and subjects alike. In the Kingdom of Heaven, the Torah (divine law) serves as the constitution, and adherence to its precepts is paramount for maintaining the orders of righteousness and justice in the kingdom. This principle highlights the inseparable connection between spiritual and political authority, and the importance of divine law in shaping the governance of the Kingdom.

The concept of sovereignty as relational power, described by political scientist Stephen D. Krasner[26], offers insights into the dynamic nature of divine sovereignty relative to the Torah-based Kingdom of Heaven on Earth. In this view, sovereignty is not just about control and domination, but about the ability to shape and influence the behavior of other actors. In the Kingdom of Heaven, divine sovereignty is expressed through acts of creation, redemption and providence[27], which establish a relational framework for interaction between YaH and creation. Inspired by the equitable nature and goodness YaH extends to Its children, the desire to be obedient increases as harmony again is established, creating an environment of shalom. Like the proper application of math formulas, this relational power shapes the covenantal relationship between YaH and humanity, giving us the impetus to carry out the principles of justice, mercy and love that manifest and govern the Kingdom for the upliftment of the cause and condition of humanity.

Transitioning to the next section of Chapter 2, we now delve into the profound significance of embodying Heaven's Principles of the Torah in our lives. The Torah, often understood as the heavenly instruction manual for living, encompasses a rich tapestry of principles and commandments that guide us toward righteousness, justice and holiness. At its core, the Torah reflects the eternal wisdom and truth of YaH, offering us a blueprint for harmonious living and spiritual fulfillment.

Rabbi Sha'ul presents a powerful Messianic perspective of the purpose of the Torah. In his letter to the household of faith, he provides the members of the community with insight into what role the Torah plays in our life as we seek to manifest the Messianic Consciousness, stating, "*...before belief came, we were being guarded under Torah, having been shut up for the belief being about to be revealed. Therefore, the Torah became our trainer unto Messiah, in order to be declared right by belief..." (Galatians 3.23-24).*

As our trainer unto Messiah, the Torah provides us with instructions for life and insights into the ways of righteousness. It is a guide that shapes our character and prepares our hearts to receive and live out the principles of Messianic Consciousness. With its commandments and teachings, the Torah serves as a mirror reflecting our shortcomings and a map directing us toward a higher standard of living.

Rabbi Sha'ul's depiction of the Torah as a guardian and trainer emphasizes its role in cultivating a disciplined and faithful life that embodies heavenly principles. The Torah's precepts are not just ancient rules, rather they are timeless principles that lead us to understand the heart and mind of the Messiah, which ultimately connects us to the heart and mind of YaH. By engaging with the Torah, we learn to align our actions and thoughts with the will of YaH, fostering a deeper relationship with our Father and King, as well as with one another.

This journey of learning and growth through the Torah is crucial for developing the belief that Rabbi Sha'ul speaks of. It is a belief that goes beyond mere intellectual acknowledgment and assent; it is an active, living faith that transforms us from within. As we internalize the teachings of the Torah, we are equipped to embody the love, justice and mercy it espouses as hallmarks of the Messianic Consciousness.

Moreover, the Torah's role as a trainer underscores the active process and dynamic nature of our spiritual journey. It acknowledges that we are intentionally engaging our becoming, continuously being reshaped, refined and renewed. The Torah challenges us to rise above our base instincts and to strive for a life that reflects the esteem and nature of the Creator. It encourages us to seek not just obedience to the letter of the law, but to embrace the spirit of the law, which is the embodiment of the power of love.

In essence, the Torah is a divine tool for personal and communal transformation. It leads us to the feet of Messiah, who embodies the fulfillment of the Torah's promises and purposes. Through the Torah, we learn what it means to walk in the footsteps of the Messiah, to live out the values of the Kingdom of YaH, and to be light and salt in a world that desperately needs hope and direction, revelation and purification.

As we continue to engage with the Torah, let us do so with open hearts and minds, ready to be shaped and guided towards the fullness of Messianic Consciousness. Let us embrace its teachings as a source of wisdom and life, leading us ever closer to the image of the Messiah. And in doing so, let us manifest the righteousness that comes from a deep and abiding faith, fulfilling our calling to be a holy and set-apart people.

Moreover, the Torah has the power to transform our hearts and minds, leading to spiritual renewal and transformation. In Deuteronomy 30:6, Moses prophesies, "*And YaH your Elohim will circumcise your heart and the heart of your offspring, so that you will love YaH your Elohim with all your heart and with all your soul, that you may live.*" This imagery of circumcision of the heart symbolizes the removal of spiritual barriers and impediments that hinder our relationship with YaH, enabling us to love and serve our Father and King wholeheartedly, in Spirit and Truth.

Not only that, but the Torah serves as a source of inspiration, comfort and guidance in times of trial and tribulation. In Deuteronomy 30:10-11, Moses reassures the Israelites that the commandments of the Torah are not too difficult to observe, nor are they beyond their reach. Rather, they are accessible and attainable, providing us with strength and resilience to overcome challenges and obstacles that we may encounter along life's journey.

Deuteronomy 30 serves as a powerful witness that illuminates the transformative power of the Torah in our lives, offering us the opportunity to choose life and blessing by learning and embracing its principles. Through study and observance, which leads to the embodiment of Torah, we experience spiritual renewal, personal growth and alignment with the heavenly will of YaH. May we heed the words of Moses and choose life by embracing the transformative power of the Torah in our lives, thinking its thoughts, walking in its ways and experiencing the abundant blessings that flow from obedience to heavenly wisdom and truth.

To arrive at a comprehensive embodiment of the Torah, we must also consider the oral tradition, as expounded upon by the sages of Israel, which provides further depth and insight into the principles of the Torah. In Pirkei Avot 1:1, it is stated, "*Moses received the Torah from Sinai and transmitted it to Joshua, and Joshua to the elders, and the elders to the prophets, and the prophets transmitted it to the men of the Great Assembly.*" This teaching highlights the unbroken chain of transmission of Torah wisdom from generation to generation, emphasizing its timeless relevance and applicability to every aspect of human life.

The Responsibility to Rule in Righteousness

As we draw near the conclusion of this chapter, it is essential to delve into the profound responsibility of ruling in righteousness, a principle deeply rooted in the Torah and exemplified by the archetypal pattern of Adam. As I have already stated, understanding and embodying Heaven's principles of rulership is not merely an intellectual exercise but a transformative journey that calls us to align our lives with heavenly wisdom and divine justice.

Hearkening back to Genesis 1.26-28, which is the divine blueprint for humanity's role as stewards of creation, it is because of that injunction that we are made in the image and likeness of Elohim and called to reflect YaH's character and attributes in our rulership. This entails ruling with wisdom, compassion, justice and humility—qualities that are central to divine governance.

To rule in righteousness, we must first internalize and embody Heaven's principles as revealed in the Torah. The Torah provides a comprehensive guide to living a life of set-apartness and justice, offering specific commandments and broader ethical teachings that shape our character and actions. Key principles include:

1. **Justice and Fairness**

The Torah emphasizes the importance of justice and fairness in all aspects of life. Deuteronomy 16:20 declares, "*Justice, justice you shall pursue, that you may live and inherit the land which YaH your Elohim is giving you.*" This repeated call to justice underscores its paramount importance in maintaining social harmony and divine favor.

2. **Compassion and Mercy**:

The Torah teaches us to care for the vulnerable and marginalized. In Exodus 22:21-22, we are commanded, "*You shall not wrong a sojourner or oppress him, for you were sojourners in the land of Egypt. You shall not mistreat any widow or fatherless child.*" This call to compassion reflects YaH's own merciful nature and our duty to emulate it.

3. **Integrity and Honesty**:

Righteous rulership requires integrity and honesty. Leviticus 19:11-12 instructs, "*You shall not steal; you shall not deal falsely; you shall not lie to one another. You shall not swear by my Name falsely, and so profane the name of your Elohim: I am YaH.*" Upholding truth and integrity fosters trust and stability within the community.

Additionally, Isaiah 11:1-4 offers a Messianic vision of righteous rulership, describing a future leadership endowed with divine wisdom and understanding: "*There shall come forth a shoot from the stump of Jesse, and a branch from his roots shall bear fruit. And the Spirit of YaH shall rest upon him, the Spirit of wisdom and understanding, the Spirit of counsel and might, the Spirit of knowledge and the fear of YaH. And his delight shall be in the fear of YaH. He shall not judge by what his eyes see, or decide disputes by what his ears hear, but with righteousness he shall judge the poor, and decide with equity for the meek of the earth.*"

Humility is a cornerstone of righteous rulership. It requires recognizing our dependence on YaH and our role as His representatives on earth. In Deuteronomy 17:18-20, the Torah prescribes that a king must write a copy of the Torah and read it all his life to learn to fear YaH, ensuring that "*his heart may not be lifted up above his brothers, and that he may not turn aside from the commandment.*" This humility keeps rulers grounded and aligned with YaH's divine will.

Applying these principles in today's context involves a commitment to justice, integrity, and compassion in all areas of leadership and influence. Whether in government, business or community roles, embodying Heaven's principles requires us to:

1. **Promote Social Justice**

Advocate for policies and practices that uphold the dignity and rights of all individuals, especially the marginalized and oppressed.

2. **Practice Ethical Leadership**

Lead with integrity, transparency and accountability, fostering environments of trust and respect.

3. **Cultivate Compassion**:

Extend kindness and support to those in need, reflecting YaH's mercy in our interactions.

4. **Embrace Humility**

Recognize our limitations and seek guidance from divine wisdom, striving to serve selflessly.

The New Testament reinforces the principles of righteousness, justice and holiness, calling all disciples to be "*children of light*" and to live lives that reflect YaH's character. Ephesians 5:8-9 powerfully exhorts, "*For at one time you were darkness, but now you are light in YaH. Walk as children of light (for the fruit of light is found in all that is good and right and true)*." This passage emphasizes the transformative journey from darkness to light, symbolizing the moral and spiritual renewal that believers undergo through their relationship with YaH.

The metaphor of light is a recurring theme in the New Testament, symbolizing truth, purity and divine revelation. Yeshua Himself declares in John 8:12, "*I am the light of the world. Whoever follows me will not walk in darkness, but will have the light of life*." As followers of Yeshua, disciples are called to reflect this divine light, becoming bearers of YaH's truth and love in a world often shrouded in spiritual darkness.

In Matthew 5:14-16, Yeshua further instructs his disciples with the Law of Equivalence of Form, "*You are the light of the world. A city set on a hill cannot be hidden. Nor do people light a lamp and put it under a basket, but on a stand, and it gives light to all in the house. In the same way, let your light shine before others, so that they may see your good works and give esteem to your Father who is in heaven*." This passage highlights the active role we as disciples play in manifesting YaH's light through our actions, serving as beacons of hope and righteousness in our families, communities and greater society. Through our reflection of the nature of YaH as the light of the world, others are drawn to our light and eventually learn to take on the characteristics we reflect of our Father and King.

In alignment with the pattern of Adam, the responsibility to rule in righteousness is a mandate of heaven for all believers. As we have covered Genesis 1:26-28 in-depth, we are now more than familiar with the outline of humanity's original calling to have dominion over creation, reflecting YaH's sovereign rule through justice and compassion. This heavenly blueprint finds its fulfillment in the life and teachings of Yeshua, who models perfect obedience to YaH's will and exemplifies the virtues of humility, love and service.

Paul echoes this mandate in Romans 13:1-4, where he teaches about the role of authority and governance: "*Let every person be subject to the governing authorities. For there is no authority except from YaH, and those that exist have been instituted by YaH...For rulers are not a terror to good conduct, but to bad...For he is YaH's servant for your good.*" Here, Paul underscores the principle that all authority derives from Elohim and must be exercised in accordance with the Torah's righteousness and justice; if it is not exercising its powers accordingly, then we, like Daniel and other righteous individuals who paid the powers that be any heed, have no responsibility to align ourselves with its corrupted leadership. Even Messiah was resistant to the corrupted powers of the priesthood and the Roman Empire, rather following the laws of Yah and letting Pontius Pilate know that, "my kingdom is not of this world."

As "children of light," disciples are called to bear the fruit of the light, which is characterized by "*all that is good and right and true*" (Ephesians 5:9). This involves a commitment to ethical living, guided by the principles of the Torah and the teachings of Yeshua. Rabbi Sha'ul provides further clarity in Galatians 5:22-23, listing the fruit of the Spirit: "*love, joy, peace, patience, kindness, goodness, faithfulness, gentleness, self-control.*" These virtues encapsulate the essence of a life lived in alignment with YaH's will, reflecting His image and likeness.

The transformative power of living as children of light is evident in the impact it has on both individuals and communities. In 1 Thessalonians 5:5, Rav Sha'ul reminds disciples, "*For you are all children of light, children of the day. We are not of the night or of the darkness.*" This identity as children of light calls disciples to a higher standard of living, one that actively resists the forces of darkness and embodies the values of YaH's kingdom.

Shimon Kepha, or Simon Peter, also addresses this theme in 1 Peter 2:9, proclaiming, "*But you are a chosen race, a royal priesthood, a holy nation, a people for his own possession, that you may proclaim the excellencies of him who called you out of darkness into his marvelous light.*" This passage emphasizes the communal aspect of living as children of light, highlighting the collective responsibility to demonstrate and proclaim YaH's esteem through righteous living.

Given the presentments of this chapter, it should be clear that our responsibility to rule in righteousness is a divine mandate that calls for us to embody Heaven's principles as revealed in the Torah and exemplified by the pattern of Adam. By pursuing justice, compassion and humility, we align ourselves with YaH's sovereign will and become agents of His Torah-based governance on earth. As children of light, we are called to shine forth with the radiance of YaH's love and truth, bringing healing and restoration to a world in need.

May we embrace this sacred responsibility with devotion and diligence, striving to reflect the image and likeness of Elohim in all that we do. By living according to the principles of the Torah and Yeshua's interpretative teachings of the Torah, we fulfill our heavenly calling and illuminate the path for others, guiding them towards the light of YaH's eternal Kingdom. Let our lives be a witness to the transformative power of hevenly light, as we walk in the footsteps of the Master, bringing forth the fruits of the Spirit and manifesting the esteem of Elohim in every aspect of our existence.

CHAPTER III
REPRODUCING THE IMAGE AND LIKENESS

Abraham and Sarah stand as monumental figures in the Israelite tradition, embodying the divine mandate to be fruitful and multiply not only through their descendants but also through their profound spiritual influence on those they encountered. The oral traditions of Israel recount with great detail how Abraham and Sarah's journey from Ur to Canaan, including their significant stop in Haran, was marked by their dedication to spreading the knowledge of the One True Elohim. This mission was a direct fulfillment of the divine command to be fruitful and multiply, as they expanded YaH's family by winning converts and establishing a community rooted in faith and righteousness.

The journey of Abraham (then Abram) and Sarah (then Sarai) begins with a divine call recorded in Genesis 12:1-3: "*YaH had said to Abram, 'Go out from your country, your people and your father's household to the land I will show you. I will make you into a great nation, and I will bless you; I will make your name great, and you will be a blessing. I will bless those who bless you, and whoever curses you I will curse and all peoples on earth will be blessed through you.*'"

The oral traditions expand on this narrative, emphasizing Abraham's role as a pioneer of the revelation of the One true and living Elohim in a predominantly idolatrous and polytheistic world. According to these traditions, Abraham was not only a seeker of YaH but also a priest and prophet. As he traveled, he engaged with people from different cultures and backgrounds, sharing the message of the One True El, inviting them to join in his covenantal journey.

One significant stop in Abraham and Sarah's journey was Haran, a place where they resided for some time before moving on to Canaan. Genesis 12:4-5 states, "*So Abram went, as YaH had told him; and Lot went with him. Abram was seventy-five years old when he set out from Haran. He took his wife Sarai, his nephew Lot, all the possessions they had accumulated and the people they had acquired in Haran, and they set out for the land of Canaan, and they arrived there.*"

The "people they had acquired" in Haran are understood by the sages to mean the converts who joined Abraham and Sarah's household. The Midrash elaborates on this, portraying Abraham as a "father of many nations" not only through physical progeny but also through spiritual offspring. Abraham and Sarah were deeply committed to their mission of spreading the awareness of YaH. They established a center of learning and hospitality, where they taught about Elohim's ways and welcomed anyone willing to learn.

The Midrash (Bereshit Rabbah 39:14) describes how Abraham would set up his tent at crossroads to offer food and shelter to travelers. His tent was open on all four sides, symbolizing his openness to all people. As guests partook in his hospitality, Abraham and Sarah would engage them in conversations about the Most High, gently guiding them away from idolatry and towards the acknowledgement and worship of the One True Elohim. This method of hospitality combined with teaching was highly effective, resulting in many converts.

Rabbinic tradition holds that Sarah played a crucial role in this mission. While Abraham taught the men, Sarah would teach the women, thus ensuring that entire families were brought into the fold of monotheism. This collaborative effort was instrumental in fulfilling the divine mandate to be fruitful and multiply, as they were not merely multiplying physically but spiritually, increasing the number of people who acknowledged and worshiped Elohim.

Abraham and Sarah's efforts are seen as a direct fulfillment of the Torah's mandate given to humanity in Genesis 1:28, "*Be fruitful and increase in number; fill the earth and subdue it*." While this command initially pertains to physical procreation, in the context of Abraham and Sarah's mission, it also encompasses spiritual multiplication. By winning converts and establishing a community devoted to Elohim, they were "filling the earth" with the knowledge of YaH and "subduing" it by spreading righteousness and justice.

The story of Abraham and Sarah's journey from Ur to Canaan, particularly their time in Haran, highlights their pivotal role in spreading the knowledge of Elohim and fulfilling the Torah's 2mandate to be fruitful and multiply. Through their unwavering faith, dedication to teaching and exceptional hospitality, they expanded the family of YaH, creating a legacy that would be foundational for the people of Israel. As we explore their story, we gain valuable insights into our own call to embody and propagate the principles of faith, righteousness and hospitality, continuing the mission of being fruitful and multiplying in both physical and spiritual realms.

UNDERSTANDING BEING FRUITFUL AND MULTIPLYING

The principle of being fruitful and multiplying is a foundational concept in the Hebrew Bible and is pregnant with not only physical allusions, but also theological, ethical and spiritual implications. This principle is further expounded upon in the New Testament and explored in depth within the Mishnah and Zohar. Drawing from these rich sources, I intend to elucidate the multifaceted nature of this divine mandate of bearing fruit and multiplying.

Being now well aware of the principle of being fruitful and multiplying relative to Adam and Chawwah, we also find this command reiterated after the Flood in Genesis 9:1, when YaH blesses Noah and his sons: "*Be fruitful and increase in number and fill the earth*." The reason for this is to re-establish the covenant with Noah's generation after the reset, reminding him and his family of the ancestral heritage of fulfilling the Torah's mandate that was first passed down to his forefather Adam.

These passages emphasize procreation as a fundamental aspect of human existence, ensuring the survival and growth of the human species. This speaks not only to the purpose of the physical gift of sexual intercourse, but also to the spiritual requirement of being witnesses of the reality of the existence of YaH. This mandate, when coupled with the command to "fill the earth and subdue it" also suggests a broader mandate to steward creation, exercise responsible dominion, and cultivate the world in harmony with divine intentions, not just for selfish gratifications.

This principle is also present in the New Testament which in the same Spirit continues to uphold the value of being fruitful, extending the concept to spiritual and communal growth. In John 15:5, Yeshua teaches, "*I am the vine*, *you are the branches*. *If you remain in me and I in you*, *you will bear much fruit*; *apart from me you can do nothing*." This passage highlights the importance of spiritual fruitfulness, which comes from abiding in Messiah. The "fruit" here refers to virtues, good works and the expansion of YaH's kingdom through discipleship and evangelism.

Furthermore, in 2 Peter 1:8 emphasizes the transformative power of cultivating virtues, as these qualities ensure that believers remain active and productive in their relationship with Yeshua Messiah. This growth in character reflects the fruitful life expected of those who truly know and follow the Master, demonstrating the living out of faith through continuous spiritual development unto perfection. Kepha wrote, "f*or if these [virtues] are in you and increase, they cause you to be neither inactive nor without fruit in the knowledge of our Master Messiah Yeshua.*"

The Mishnah also offers additional insights into the principle of being fruitful and multiplying. In Pirkei Avot 4:2, it is stated, *"Ben Azzai said: Be quick in performing a minor commandment as in the case of a major one and flee from transgression. For one commandment leads to another commandment, and transgression leads to another transgression. For the reward for performing a commandment is another commandment and the reward for committing a transgression is a transgression."* This lesson teaches us that the work we sow in life reaps the same in kind based on the energy that we use to produce the outcome. If we are fruitful in obeying the Word of Elohim, we will produce more obedience. If we are rebellious and intent on living a life of unrighteousness, however, we will only become more corrupt.

This is also confirmed in the Messianic Scriptures where John the Revelator reveals the exhortation of the Master Messiah Yeshua to his readers, "*He who does wrong, let him do more wrong; he who is filthy, let him be more filthy; he who is righteous, let him be more righteous; he who is set-apart, let him be more set-apart*" (Revelation 22.11).

Pirkei Avot 5:21 also advises, "*At five years old, one is fit for the study of Scripture, at ten for the study of Mishnah, at thirteen for the obligation of the commandments, at fifteen for the study of Talmud, at eighteen for marriage...*" This teaching emphasizes the importance of education, moral development and the establishment of families as part of fulfilling the command to be fruitful and multiply. It shows a structured approach to personal and communal growth that aligns with divine commandments.

Kabbalistic literature, particularly the Zohar, provides a mystical dimension to the principle of being fruitful and multiplying, interpreting the physical and spiritual aspects of this command. In Zohar 1:4b, it is written, "*When the Blessed Holy One created Adam, He formed him from the dust of the ground, gathered from the four corners of the earth, and breathed into his nostrils the breath of life, planting within him a soul from the upper worlds.*" This passage highlights the dual nature of humanity, combining earthly and divine elements, and suggests that being fruitful involves nurturing both physical and spiritual life.

Furthermore, the Zohar 3:79a explains that the command to be fruitful and multiply extends to the proliferation of divine wisdom and holiness in the world. "*Just as the human body must be fruitful and multiply, so must the soul increase in wisdom and understanding, spreading the light of the Shekinah Presence throughout creation.*" This mystical interpretation connects physical procreation with spiritual enlightenment and the dissemination of divine knowledge.

By synthesizing these perspectives, we are able to more fully appreciate the comprehensive nature of the principle of being fruitful and multiplying. This principle encompasses:

1. **Physical Procreation**: Ensuring the continuation of the human species through the establishment of families and communities. This aspect is foundational and is emphasized in the Genesis accounts.

2. **Spiritual Fruitfulness**: Cultivating virtues and ethical behaviors that reflect the divine image. The New Testament focuses on spiritual growth and the manifestation of the "fruit of the Spirit."

3. **Individual and Communal Intellectual Growth**: Transmitting Torah knowledge and ethical teachings across generations, as highlighted in the Mishnah. This ensures the preservation and flourishing of divine wisdom and moral values. We read of this powerful dynamic in the book of Acts in relation to the growth of the Gentile righteous converts, when James, the Prince of the Nazarene community and brother of Messiah Yeshua states, *"For from ancient generations Mosheh has, in every city, those proclaiming him – being read in the congregations every Sabbath"* (Acts 15.21). The Bereans in Thessalonica, mentioned in Acts 17.10-11, also demonstrate individual and collective study; "*these [Bereans] were more noble than those in Thessalonike, who received the word with great eagerness, and searched the Scriptures daily, if these words were so.*"

4. **Mystical Enlightenment**: Expanding the Shekinah Presence and wisdom of the Torah in the world, as described in the Zohar,

involves a deeper spiritual awakening and the proliferation of holiness and divine light. The words of the Master Yeshua resonate with this matter with his extension of the Great Commission, stating, "*go and make taught ones of all the nations*, *immersing them in the Name of the Father and of the Son and of the Set-apart Spirit*, *teaching them to guard all that I have commanded you*. *And see*, *I am with you always*, *until the end of the age*" (Matthew 28.19-20).

Reflecting on these passages, it should be apparent to see that the command to be fruitful and multiply is a multi-dimensional principle that encompasses physical, spiritual, educational and mystical growth. It calls for humanity to not only populate the earth but also to fill it with righteousness, wisdom and the Shekinah Presence of YaH. As we strive to embody this principle, may we righteously fulfill our role as bearers of YaH's image, contributing to the flourishing of creation and the realization of YaH's Kingdom of Heaven on Earth. Through the teachings of the Hebrew Bible, the Messianic Scriptures, Mishnah and Zohar, we gain a holistic understanding of this divine mandate, inspiring us to live lives that are fruitful in every sense of the word.

HOW TO BECOME FRUITFUL AND MULTIPLY

Being fruitful and multiplying in the fullest sense requires a deep commitment to guarding the covenant, obeying the commandments, practicing selflessness and embodying love for YaH and humanity. This section will explore these principles in depth, drawing from a broad spectrum of sacred texts, continuing the use of references from the Hebrew and Messianic Scriptures, the oral tradition of the Mishnah, the mystical insights of the Zohar and now utilizing additional wisdom from the Apocrypha and Pseudepigrapha.

The concept of guarding the covenant is central to the Hebrew and Messianic Scriptures. In Genesis 17:9-10, Elohim commands Abraham, "*As for you, you must keep my covenant, you and your descendants after you for the generations to come. This is my covenant with you and your descendants after you, the covenant you are to keep: Every male among you shall be circumcised.*" This act of circumcision is a physical sign of a deeper spiritual commitment to uphold YaH's commandments and live according to Its will.

In fact, the ritual of circumcision has as its intent the removal of the kelipot of which we spoke earlier. The rite of circumcision is a matter of initiating the transformational process of going from mortal to immortal; from corrupt to incorruption; from earthly to heavenly. Symbolizing the spiritual dynamic of the circumcision of the heart, or the removal of the foreskin of flesh, the circumcision truly reveals the principle of being sensitized to the spirit of YaH after one sets aside the excessive nature of the flesh, which allows for them to observe and guard the covenant of YaH.

The idea of guarding the covenant, however, extends beyond physical rituals to encompass a holistic dedication to living a life that honors YaH. Deuteronomy 11:1 underscores this broader commitment: "*Love YaH your Elohim and keep his charge, his decrees, his laws and his commands always.*"

In the New Testament, this principle is echoed in passages such as John 14:15, where Yeshua states, "*If you love me, keep my commands.*" This demonstrates that true love for Elohim is manifested through obedience and faithfulness to His teachings. This principle is first echoed in the Torah where YaH speaks to Moses in regard to the giving of the ten commandments at Exodus 20.4-6: "*You do not make for yourself a carved image, or any likeness of that which is in the heavens above, or which is in the earth beneath, or which is in the waters under the earth, you do not bow down to them nor serve them. For I, יהוה your Elohim am a jealous Ěl, visiting the crookedness of the fathers on the children to the third and fourth generations of those who hate Me, but showing kindness to thousands,* ***to those who love Me and guard My commands***."

The Mishnah further emphasizes the importance of safeguarding the covenant. In Pirkei Avot 3:17, it states, "*Without the fear of heaven, there can be no wisdom; without wisdom, there can be no fear of heaven.*" This highlights the interdependence of reverence for YaH and the pursuit of divine wisdom, both of which are essential for guarding the covenant. In this sense fear is relative to awe and reverence, and not the type of fear that we associate with fright and terror.

The Zohar also provides a mystical dimension to this principle. In Zohar 1:88a, it is written, "*The covenant is the foundation of all holiness and purity. Those who guard the covenant are the ones who bring forth light and blessings into the world.*" This mystical interpretation connects the physical act of circumcision with a broader spiritual responsibility to uphold divine principles.

FAITHFULNESS TO THE COMMANDMENTS

Faithfulness to YaH's commandments is integral to being fruitful and multiplying in a way that aligns our attention with divine purpose. Deuteronomy 6:6-7 instructs, "*These commandments that I give you today are to be on your hearts. Impress them on your children. Talk about them when you sit at home and when you walk along the road, when you lie down and when you get up.*" This passage emphasizes the importance of internalizing and teaching YaH's laws, ensuring that they permeate every aspect of life. Looking at the order of the process, it starts with self, extends to family and then goes beyond.

In the New Testament, faithfulness is presented as a hallmark of genuine discipleship. In Matthew 22:37-40, Yeshua summarizes the commandments with the dual command to love Elohim and love your neighbor: "'*Love YaH your Elohim with all your heart and with all your soul and with all your mind*.' *This is the first and greatest commandment*. *And the second is like it*: '*Love your neighbor as yourself*.' *All the Law and the Prophets hang on these two commandments*." Quoting passages from the Torah, Deuteronomy 6.5 and Leviticus 19.18, respectively, Yeshua places the act of love in the realm of intellectual acknowledgement and righteous conduct. For it is when the heart and mind are aligned and functioning together, humanity is operating at its highest capacity.

The Mishnah also stresses the importance of obedience. In Pirkei Avot 2:1, Rabbi Yehuda Ha Nasi teaches, "*Be as meticulous in observing a minor commandment as a major one, for you do not know the reward for each commandment.*" This suggests that every commandment, regardless of perceived significance, is vital to a life of righteousness.

The Zohar elaborates on the spiritual significance of the commandments. In Zohar 2:86b, it is written, "*The commandments are the channels through which divine light flows into the world. Each act of obedience opens a gate for blessing and sanctity.*" This mystical perspective highlights how following YaH's laws is not just an obligation but a means of bringing the Shekinah presence of YaH into the world.

Selfless love is a foundational virtue in the pursuit of being fruitful and multiplying. This call to love others is central to the ethical teachings of the Hebrew Scriptures. In the New Testament, Yeshua amplifies this principle in John 13:34-35: "*A new command I give you: Love one another. As I have loved you, so you must love one another. By this everyone will know that you are my disciples, if you love one another.*" This passage underscores the transformative power of love and its role in identifying true disciples of Messiah.

The Mishnah reinforces the importance of selfless love. In Pirkei Avot 1:12, Rabbi Hillel teaches, "*Be of the disciples of Aaron, loving peace and pursuing peace, loving your fellow creatures, and drawing them near to the Torah.*" This highlights the role of love in fostering community and guiding others towards divine truth.

The Zohar delves deeper into the spiritual dynamics of love. In Zohar 3:140b, it states, "*Love is the root of all commandments. It is through love that the soul is united with [YaH] and with all creation.*" This mystical interpretation emphasizes that love is the essence of spiritual fulfillment and connection with YaH.

The Apocrypha and Pseudepigrapha offer additional perspectives on these principles. The Book of Sirach (Ecclesiasticus) 2:6-9 advises, "*Trust in him, and he will help you; make your ways straight, and hope in him. You who fear YaH, wait for his mercy, and turn not aside, lest you fall. You who fear YaH, trust in him, and your reward will not fail.*" This passage highlights the importance of trust and obedience in maintaining a righteous life.

In the Pseudepigrapha, the Book of Jubilees 20:1-2 recounts Abraham's instructions to his children, emphasizing obedience and love: "*And Abraham said to his son Isaac, 'I am old, and know not the day of my death, and am full of my days. And behold, I am one hundred and seventy-five years old, and throughout all the days of my life I have remembered YaH and sought with all my heart to do his will, and to walk uprightly in all his ways.'*"

Understanding and embodying the principle of being fruitful and multiplying involves a comprehensive commitment to guarding the covenant, obeying YaH's commandments, practicing selfless love for YaH and humanity. This divine mandate is intricately woven through the fabric of Scripture and oral traditions, offering a holistic path to spiritual and communal growth. As we align our lives with these principles, we fulfill our heavenly purpose, becoming channels of YaH's light and love in the world. Through the teachings of the Hebrew Scriptures, the New Testament, the Mishnah, the Zohar, and other sacred texts, we gain a profound understanding of how to live and cultivate a life that truly reflects the image and likeness of Elohim.

Cultivating Spiritual Fertility

Cultivating spiritual fertility involves nurturing the inner qualities and virtues that allow for the growth and flourishing of one's spiritual life. This process is richly described in the Sefer Yetzirah and the Mishnah. By understanding these teachings and integrating them with scientific explanations, we can gain a comprehensive view of how to cultivate a spiritually fertile life.

The Sefer Yetzirah, one of the foundational texts of Kabbalistic thought, provides a mystical framework for understanding spiritual fertility. The text outlines the process of creation through the manipulation of the Hebrew letters and the ten sefirot, or divine emanations. In Sefer Yetzirah 1:1, it states, "*By means of thirty-two wonderful paths of wisdom, Yah, the Master of hosts, the Elohim of Israel, the living El, King of the universe, El Shaddai, Merciful and Kind, High and Exalted, dwelling in eternity, whose name is Holy – He is lofty and holy – He created His universe.*"

This mystical creation process can be seen as a metaphor for spiritual cultivation. Just as Elohim used wisdom and divine emanations to create the world, individuals can cultivate spiritual fertility by engaging in practices that align them with divine wisdom and the sefirot. This involves meditative practices, prayer, and the study of sacred texts, which help to align one's inner life with the divine structure of the universe.

Teachings from the Mishnah

The Mishnah provides practical guidance on how to live a life that fosters spiritual fertility. In Pirkei Avot 1:2, it states, "*The world stands on three things: on Torah, on service and on acts of lovingkindness.*" These three pillars represent the essential practices that cultivate a spiritually fertile life.

1. **Torah**: Engaging in the study and application of Torah helps individuals to align their lives with the wisdom and commandments of YaH. This practice fosters spiritual growth by providing a framework for ethical and moral living.

2. **Service**: Serving YaH through prayer and ritual observance cultivates a deep connection with YaH. This service, coupled with a heart of devotion, nurtures the soul and promotes spiritual flourishing.

3. **Acts of Lovingkindness**: Practicing kindness and compassion towards others is a tangible expression of spiritual fertility. These acts not only benefit the recipient but also enrich the giver's spiritual life by fostering a heart of empathy and love.

Scientific Explanations

From a scientific perspective, cultivating spiritual fertility can be understood through the lens of positive psychology[28], which studies the factors that contribute to human flourishing. Research has shown that practices such as mindfulness, gratitude and altruism significantly enhance well-being and promote personal growth.

Mindfulness, a practice of focused attention and awareness, has been shown to increase emotional regulation and reduce stress. This aligns with the spiritual practices of prayer and meditation found in spiritual traditions, which aim to cultivate a peaceful and centered inner life.

Gratitude, the practice of recognizing and appreciating the good in life, is another key factor in fostering spiritual fertility. Studies have shown that gratitude enhances emotional well-being and promotes positive social interactions. This practice resonates with the biblical emphasis on thanksgiving and praise as seen in passages like Psalm 100:4, "*Enter his gates with thanksgiving and his courts with praise; give thanks to him and praise his name.*"

Altruism, or selfless concern for the well-being of others, is closely related to the concept of acts of lovingkindness in the Mishnah. Research indicates that engaging in altruistic behaviors increases life satisfaction and emotional well-being, supporting the idea that spiritual fertility involves nurturing positive relationships and contributing to the welfare of others.

Integrative Understanding

By integrating the teachings from the Sefer Yetzirah, the Mishnah and scientific research, we can develop a holistic approach to cultivating spiritual fertility. This involves:

1. **Connection with YaH**: Maintaining a deep and abiding relationship with YaH through prayer, meditation and the study of sacred texts. This connection is the foundation of spiritual fertility, as emphasized by Yeshua in John 15:5.

2. **Engagement with Sacred Wisdom of Torah**: Regularly studying and applying the teachings of the Torah and other sacred texts to align one's life with divine principles. This practice nurtures the soul and promotes ethical and moral growth, transforming us from "esteem to esteem," so that our thoughts and ways become the thoughts and ways of YaH.

3. **Service and Devotion**: Participating in religious services and rituals that foster a connection with YaH and cultivate a heart of devotion. This service enhances spiritual fertility by deepening one's relationship with Elohim.

4. **Acts of Lovingkindness**: Practicing compassion and kindness towards others, reflecting the divine attribute of chesed (lovingkindness). These acts not only benefit others but also enrich the giver's spiritual life.

5. **Mindfulness and Gratitude**: Incorporating mindfulness and gratitude practices to enhance emotional well-being and promote a positive outlook on life. These practices align with the biblical emphasis on thanksgiving and praise.

Cultivating spiritual fertility is a multifaceted endeavor that involves nurturing one's inner life through a deep connection with YaH, engagement with the Torah and the practice of love and kindness towards others. By drawing from the rich teachings of the Hebrew and Messianic Scriptures, the Sefer Yetzirah, the Mishnah, and scientific research, we can develop a comprehensive approach to spiritual growth that reflects the fullness of the image and likeness of YaH within us. Through these practices, we fulfill the Torah's mandate to be fruitful and multiply, contributing to the flourishing of creation and the realization of YaH's Kingdom of Heaven on Earth.

CHAPTER IV
THE RESURRECTION OF ADAM

"You are mighty forever, my Master; You resurrect the dead; You are powerful to save. He causes the dew to descend. You sustain the living with loving kindness, resurrect the dead with great mercy, support the falling, heal the sick, release the bound, and fulfill Your trust with those who sleep in the dust. Who is like You, Elohim! And who can be compared to You, King, who brings death and restores life, and causes deliverance to spring forth! For You are trustworthy to revive the dead. Blessed are You YaH, who revives the dead. Amein[29]."

- Excerpt from the Amidah prayer -

The concept of resurrection, known as *techiyat hametim* in Hebrew, is a cornerstone of Israelite ideology, intricately interwoven into the foundational understanding and fabric of our perspectives of faith and events pertaining to the end times redemption of Israel and humanity. As one of the Thirteen Principles of Faith identified by Maimonides, the principle of resurrection is a fundamental tenet of the heavenly revealed order of creation. This section of the chapter will delve into the rabbinic and Messianic perspectives of resurrection, elucidating its spiritual, mental and physical dimensions, relating these ideas to the pattern of Adam and humanity's return to our primordial nature.

1. **Spiritual Resurrection**

From a spiritual standpoint, the resurrection signifies the renewal and elevation of the soul. It is a return to a state of purity and closeness to YaH, as seen in the promise of redemption and eternal life. In the Hebrew Scriptures, the prophet Daniel speaks of a time when "*many of those who sleep in the dust of the earth shall awake, some to everlasting life and some to shame and everlasting contempt*" (Daniel 12:2). This suggests a future awakening where souls are judged and rewarded or punished, indicating a restoration of spiritual alignment with YaH's will.

In the Messianic Scriptures Yeshua speaks of the resurrection in spiritual terms: "*I am the resurrection and the life. The one who believes in me will live, even though they die*" (John 11:25). This highlights belief and faithfulness as essential components of spiritual resurrection.

2. **Mental Resurrection**

Mental resurrection involves the transformation and renewal of the mind, aligning one's thoughts and intentions with divine principles. This cognitive renewal is essential for living a righteous and fulfilling life according to YaH's commandments.

In the Hebrew Scriptures the prophet Ezekiel's vision of the dry bones represents a renewal of the mind and spirit: "*I will put my Spirit within you, and you shall live, and I will place you in your own land*" (Ezekiel 37:14). Here, resurrection is tied to the rejuvenation of the mind and spirit.

In the Mishnah, Sanhedrin 90a: The Talmud discusses the belief in resurrection, emphasizing the renewal of knowledge and wisdom. It states, "*All Israel have a share in the world to come, for it is written: Your people also shall be all righteous; they shall inherit the land forever; the branch of My planting, the work of My hands, that I may be esteemed*" (Isaiah 60:21). This indicates a collective mental and spiritual resurrection leading to eternal life.

3. **Physical Resurrection**

Physical resurrection is the literal raising of the body from the dead, a belief that underscores the Israelite view of bodily sanctity and the integral unity of body and soul.

In the Hebrew Scriptures the prophet Isaiah speaks of the body's resurrection where he prophesies, "*Your dead shall live; their bodies shall rise. You who dwell in the dust, awake and sing for joy!*" (Isaiah 26:19). This vividly describes the physical resurrection of the dead, reflecting a future where the body is restored to life.

The Messianic Scriptures has Yeshua's resurrection as the quintessential example of physical resurrection: "*He is not here; he has risen, just as he said*" (Matthew 28:6). His bodily resurrection serves as a prototype for the future resurrection of the faithful.

With the Mishnah, at Sanhedrin 90a, the Talmud explicitly affirms the belief in bodily resurrection, stating, "*These are they that have no share in the world to come: he who says that the resurrection of the dead is a teaching which does not derive from the Torah.*" This assertion solidifies the physical resurrection as a core tenet of Israelite faith.

Adam and Humanity's Return to Primordial Nature

The narrative of Adam's creation and fall provides a profound framework for understanding the reality of resurrection. Adam's original state in the Garden of Eden was one of purity and direct communion with YaH, a state marred by sin and expulsion from Eden. Resurrection, in its spiritual, mental and physical aspects, is understood as a return to this primordial state. Just as Adam was formed from the dust and endowed with the breath of life, so too will humanity be resurrected from the dust, renewed in spirit and body. The creation account in Genesis emphasizes this connection:

"*Then YHWH Elohim formed man of the dust from the ground and breathed into his nostrils the breath of life; and man became a living being*" (Genesis 2:7). The resurrection mirrors this act of creation, a divine reformation of body, mind and spirit. The breathing of the breath of life into the nostrils of Adam was a symbolic act of the awakening of consciousness to the reality of YaH. As the passageway that leads directly to the brain, it is similar in principle to the essence of what King Solomon writes in Song of Songs 1.2a, *"let him kiss me with the kisses of his mouth..."* Representing the transmission of knowledge, this is also demonstrated in John 20.21-22, "*Then Yeshua said to them again, "'Peace to you! As the Father has sent Me, I also send you.' And having said this, He breathed on them, and said to them, 'Receive the Set-apart Spirit.'"*

Coupled with this dynamic from the creation of man, rabbi Sha'ul's writings in the Messianic Scriptures reflect this theme: "*For as in Adam all die, so in Messiah all will be made alive*" (1 Corinthians 15:22). This passage connects the resurrection to the redemption from the fall of Adam, promising a restoration to an Edenic state.

The resurrection of the dead encapsulates a profound renewal and return to our primordial nature, encompassing spiritual, mental and physical dimensions. This hope is deeply rooted in Israelite tradition and scripture, affirming a future where the faithful are restored to their intended state of holiness and communion with YaH.

Experiencing the Resurrection

The journey towards resurrection and returning to our primordial nature involves a profound transformation grounded in the principles of Torah and exemplified by pivotal events in the life of Yeshua. One such event is the Mount of Transfiguration, where Moses and Elijah appear with Yeshua, revealing a glimpse of the esteemed state to which disciples can aspire. Transfiguration is defined as a change in form or appearance; metamorphosis; an exalting, esteeming or spiritual change. Relative to change, the Hebrew word sana (שָׁנָא) *implies alteration and the release of wisdom previously held in capsule form unfolding the goal and structuring the appearance of Light.*[30]

The Mount of Transfiguration provides a powerful image of resurrection and the return to a primordial, esteemed state. The event is described in the Witness of Matthew:

"*After six days Yeshua took with him Kepha (Peter), Ya'aqob (James) and Yohanan (John) the brother of Ya'aqob and led them up a high mountain by themselves. There he was transfigured before them. His face shone like the sun, and his clothes became as white as the light. Just then there appeared before them Moses and Elijah, talking with Yeshua*" (Matthew 17:1-3).

This passage shows Yeshua in an esteemed state, conversing with Moses and Elijah, who themselves represent the Law and the Prophets. The presence of these key figures signifies the continuity of YaH's plan from the Torah to the Messianic fulfillment. Additionally, it also suggests that these three men were initiates in the mysteries of the Torah, and more expressly what is called Ma'aseh Merkabah, or the work of the chariot. This section will explore how to undergo this transformation, highlighting the spiritual, mental and physical aspects drawing on scriptural references for deeper comprehension.

Kabbalistic Interpretation

From a Kabbalistic perspective, this passage is rich with symbolism and deeper spiritual meanings. As Kabbalah seeks to uncover the hidden aspects of YaH and the universe, let us consider the key elements of this passage and their interpretations relative to the resurrection:

1. **The High Mountain**

- *Symbol of Ascent*: Mountains in Kabbalah often symbolize a journey towards higher spiritual states. The high mountain in this setting signifies an ascent to a place of divine revelation, representing the sefirah (divine emanation) of Keter (Crown), which is the highest point of divine consciousness and unity with Elohim. It is at our peaks of consciousness that we are able to experience resurrection and enter into the higher heights of life, as well as manifest the oneness of YaH.

2. **The Transfiguration**

- *Light and Esteem*: Yeshua's transfiguration, where His face shone like the sun and His clothes became white as light, represents a profound revelation of the divine light. This is akin to the concept of the *Ohr Ein Sof*[31] (Infinite Light), which is the pure, unbounded light of Elohim used to bring creation into manifestation. The transfiguration reveals Yeshua as a vessel of this divine light, embodying the sefirah of Tiferet (Beauty), which balances and harmonizes divine judgment and mercy.

3. **Moses and Elijah**

- *Moses (Chochmah) and Elijah (Binah)*: In Kabbalistic tradition, Moses and Elijah represent significant spiritual archetypes. Moses is often associated with the sefirah of Chochmah (Wisdom), the initial flash of insight and divine inspiration. Elijah, known for his role as a prophet who challenges with , can be associated with Binah (Understanding), the deep comprehension and formulation of wisdom. Together, they symbolize the fullness of Torah wisdom and prophetic insight, now centered on Yeshua as the ultimate Messianic revelation.

MESSIANIC INTERPRETATION

From a Messianic perspective, the Transfiguration event is seen as a pivotal moment that highlights Yeshua's divine nature and His fulfillment of both the Torah (Law) and the Prophets. Here are key elements and their interpretations:

1. **The High Mountain**

- *Place of Revelation*: In the Messianic understanding, the high mountain is reminiscent of Mount Sinai, where Moses received the Torah, and Mount Carmel, where Elijah confronted the prophets of Baal for the revelation of the supremacy of YaH. This setting underscores the continuity and fulfillment of divine revelation in Yeshua.

2. **The Transfiguration**

- *Divine Confirmation*: The transfiguration demonstrates Yeshua's divine esteem and His role as the Messiah. The radiant light symbolizes the Shekinah Presence, affirming Yeshua's identity and mission. This event echoes Daniel 7:13-14, where the "Son of Adam" is given authority and esteem by Elohim.

3. **Moses and Elijah**

- *<u>Law and Prophets</u>*: Moses represents the Torah (Law), and Elijah represents the Prophets. Their appearance with Yeshua signifies that He is the culmination and fulfillment of both the Law and the Prophets, as Yeshua himself stated "*Do not think that I have come to abolish the Law or the Prophets; I have not come to abolish them but to fulfill them*" (Matthew 5:17). This is further confirmed by Romans 10.4 which states, "*For Messiah is the goal of the 'Torah unto righteousness' to everyone who believes.*"

- *<u>Messianic Fulfillment</u>*: The presence of Moses and Elijah also points to the eschatological role of Yeshua. In Israelite tradition, Elijah is expected to return before the coming of the Messiah (Malachi 4:5-6). Their appearance together with Yeshua highlights that He is indeed the expected Messiah who brings the ultimate redemption.

By integrating these perspectives, the transfiguration can be seen as a profound revelation of Yeshua's divine and messianic identity. It represents a moment where the divine light, wisdom, and understanding (Chochmah and Binah) are fully embodied in Yeshua, harmonized through Tiferet (beauty). This event fulfills the prophecies and the Torah, affirming Yeshua as the central figure of redemption and the ultimate revelation of YaH's light to humanity.

In this unified view, the transfiguration is not just a miraculous event but a pivotal point in the spiritual history of humanity, one where the hidden aspects of Elohim as revealed by Kabbalah and the Messianic expectations converge in Yeshua, pointing to the ultimate destiny for humanity. This reveals a pathway for disciples to aspire towards their own spiritual ascent and transformation, aiming to reflect the divine light and wisdom exemplified in Yeshua.

1. **Spiritual Transformation**

Spiritual transformation is the first step in the process of resurrection. It involves repentance, faith in Yeshua, and living in accordance with YaH's commandments.

- *Repentance and Faith*: The journey begins with repentance and accepting Yeshua as the Messiah. Yohanan (John) the Baptist and Yeshua both preached the necessity of repentance: "*Repent, for the kingdom of heaven is at hand*" (Matthew 3:2, 4:17).

- *Living According to Torah*: Embracing the teachings of Torah and striving to live a righteous life is crucial. Yeshua emphasized the importance of the Torah and following his example and teachings, stating "*I am the vine, you are the branches. He who stays in Me, and I in him, he bears much fruit. Because without Me you are able to do naught! If anyone does not stay in Me, he is thrown away as a branch and dries up. And they gather them and throw them into the fire, and they are burned. If you stay in Me, and My Words stay in you, you shall ask whatever you wish, and it shall be done for you. In this My Father is esteemed, that you bear much fruit, and you shall be My taught ones. As the Father has loved Me, I have also loved you. Stay in My love. If you guard My commands, you shall stay in My love, even as I have guarded My Father's commands and stay in His love.*" (John 15.5-10).

As fruit is regularly used as a literary device to connote behavior, it is the fruit of righteousness that is produced from faithfulness which leads to eternal life, resulting from the resurrection of consciousness and our primordial nature.

2. **Mental Renewal**

Mental renewal involves the transformation of our minds to align with YaH's will, resulting in a deeper understanding of His truths and purposes.

- *Renewal of the Mind*: Paul the Apostle encourages believers to undergo a mental transformation: "*Do not conform to the pattern of this world, but be transformed by the renewing of your mind. Then you will be able to test and approve what Elohim's will is—his good, pleasing and perfect will*" (Romans 12:2).

- *Embracing Divine Wisdom*: The wisdom found in the Torah and the teachings of Yeshua guides believers towards a renewed mind, filled with heavenly discernment and understanding. We find this best expressed with these words from the Master; "*And know this, that if the master of the house had known what hour the thief would come, he would have watched and not allowed his house to be broken into. Because of this, be ready too, for the Son of Aḏam is coming at an hour when you do not expect Him. Who then is a trustworthy and wise servant, whom his master set over his household, to give them food in season? Blessed is that servant whom his master, having come, shall find so doing.* Truly, I say to you that he shall set him over all his possessions." (Matthew 24.43-47).

3. **Physical Transformation**

The final aspect is the physical transformation, which will be fully realized in the resurrection at the end of days. This transformation is a return to the esteemed state intended for humanity, as seen in the transfigured Yeshua.

- *Resurrection of the Body*: Paul describes the resurrection body as imperishable and esteemed: "*So will it be with the resurrection of the dead. The body that is sown is perishable, it is raised imperishable; it is sown in dishonor, it is raised in honor; it is sown in weakness, it is raised in power; it is sown a natural body, it is raised a spiritual body*" (1 Corinthians 15:42-44).

- *Promise of Eternal Life*: Belief in Yeshua and adherence to his teachings assure believers of eternal life and participation in the resurrection: "Yeshua said to her, '*I am the resurrection and the life. The one who believes in me will live, even though they die; and whoever lives by believing in me will never die. Do you believe this*?'" (John 11:25-26).

The process of resurrection and transformation is inherently connected to the concept of returning to our primordial nature, as exemplified by Adam before the fall. This state is characterized by purity, direct communion with Elohim, and a life free from sin and death.

1. **Restoration of Divine Image**

- *Original Purity*: Humanity was created in the image of Elohim, endowed with purity and righteousness. The fall of Adam marred this image, introducing sin and death. The resurrection restores believers to this original state of purity: "*For as in Adam all die, so in Messiah all will be made alive*" (1 Corinthians 15:22).

2. **Eternal Communion with Elohim**

- *Direct Relationship*: The esteemed state involves an intimate, unbroken relationship with Elohim, similar to the communion Adam enjoyed in the Garden of Eden. This is a return to the intended harmonious existence with our Creator: "*Now the dwelling of Elohim is with men, and he will live with them. They will be his people, and YaH himself will be with them and be their Elohim*" (Revelation 21:3).

The journey toward resurrection and the return to our primordial nature is a transformative process involving spiritual, mental and physical renewal. Rooted in the principles of Torah and exemplified by the event of the Mount of Transfiguration, this journey aligns believers with the Torah's plan of prophetic redemption and restoration. Through repentance, faith in Yeshua, adherence to Torah, and the renewal of mind and body, disciples aspire to the esteemed state of consciousness that reflects the purity and communion with Elohim intended from the beginning. This transformation is not only a return to the state of Adam before the fall but also a fulfillment of the divine promise of eternal life and resurrection in Yeshua.

The concept of dew, tal/טַל in Hebrew, holds significant mystical and theological importance within Israelite tradition, particularly in relation to resurrection. Dew is not merely a natural phenomenon but is imbued with profound spiritual symbolism, as evidenced in the Torah, the Mishnah and the Zohar. This section will explore the mystery of dew and its association with resurrection, drawing on these foundational texts.

Looking at the Hebrew spelling of the word, we find that the two letters that compose the word tal have a meaning of the consummate mark of continuity (טַ) derived from instruction that begins with enlightenment and ends in holiness (ל). From this we see how this holy, symbolic substance provides resuscitating powers to the souls who are extended the blessing from YaH El Olam.

The Torah provides the initial framework for understanding the significance of dew. It appears in various contexts, often symbolizing divine blessing and life-sustaining provision.

1. **Dew as a Blessing**

- Genesis 27:28: "*May Elohim give you heaven's dew and earth's richness—an abundance of grain and new wine.*"

This blessing, given by Isaac to Jacob, associates dew with resurrected life, but also heavenly favor and abundance. Dew, falling gently and sustaining the earth, is seen as a manifestation of YaH's nurturing presence and promise of everlasting life.

2. **Dew and Manna**

- Exodus 16:13-14: "*In the evening quail came and covered the camp, and in the morning there was a layer of dew around the camp. When the dew was gone, thin flakes like frost on the ground appeared on the desert floor.*"

The appearance of manna, the miraculous food that sustained the Israelites in the desert, is directly linked to dew. This connection underscores dew's role as a conduit of divine sustenance and life.

Dew in the Mishnah

The Mishnah, the foundational text of the Oral Torah, further elaborates on the cosmological significance of dew, particularly in relation to resurrection.

1. **Dew and Resurrection**

- Berakhot 5:2: "*Rabbi Eliezer says: He who recites the Shema and fails to mention 'True and Firm' in the morning and 'True and Trustworthy' in the evening has not fulfilled his obligation. Rabbi Yehoshua says: It is sufficient if he mentions 'Redemption' as he finishes.*" This passage highlights the importance of recognizing the power of prophetic redemption, which, according to rabbinic tradition, is intimately connected with resurrection. The idea of resurrection is often associated with the renewal and life-giving power symbolized by dew. The belief in resurrection is a core tenet of Israelite cosmology, and the Mishnah affirms its foundation in the Torah. Dew, in this context, is seen as an element through which resurrection will be actualized.

Dew in the Zohar

The Zohar, the central work of Kabbalah, delves deeply into the mystical dimensions of dew, offering profound insights into its esoteric significance and its connection to resurrection.

1. **The Dew of Heaven**

- *Zohar III, 19b* states that "*The dew of heaven refers to the secret of the divine light that descends and vivifies the Garden of Eden. This dew will awaken the dead in the time to come.*" The Zohar identifies dew with the divine light, a spiritual essence that sustains and enlivens all creation. This divine dew is seen as the agent of resurrection, capable of reanimating the dead.

2. Dew and the Tree of Life

- <u>*Zohar I, 142a*</u> informs us of how "*The Holy One, blessed be He, will rouse the dead and raise them from the dust. He will pour upon them His dew, and they will come to life, as it is written: 'Your dead will live, their bodies will rise. You who dwell in the dust, wake up and shout for joy. Your dew is like the dew of the morning; the earth will give birth to her dead*' (Isaiah 26:19)." As we previously cited this passage, it is one that explicitly connects the resurrection with dew, describing it as the means by which YaH will revive the dead. The dew is equated with the divine influence that emanates from the Tree of Life, which nourishes and revitalizes the soul.

The Esoteric Significance of Dew

1. **Dew and the Shekhinah**

The Shekhinah, the presence of YaH, is often associated with dew in Kabbalistic literature. Dew symbolizes the gentle and nurturing aspect of the Shekhinah that sustains and revives the souls of the righteous.

- <u>*Song of Songs 5:2*</u> states "*I slept but my heart was awake. Listen! My beloved is knocking: 'Open to me, my sister, my darling, my dove, my flawless one. My head is drenched with dew, my hair with the dampness of the night.'*" In this mystical interpretation, the beloved represents the Shekhinah, whose presence brings spiritual dew, reviving the soul and preparing it for the ultimate resurrection.

As has just been shown, the mystery of dew, or tal, in Israelite tradition is profoundly connected to the concept of resurrection. As elucidated in the Torah, the Mishnah, and the Zohar, dew symbolizes blessing, sustenance, and the life-giving power of Elohim. It is seen as a conduit through which the dead will be revived in the prophetic future, embodying the gentle, nurturing, and vivifying aspects of the Shekinah Presence. By understanding the multifaceted significance of dew, one gains deeper insight into the Israelite vision of resurrection and the ultimate renewal of life.

As we conclude this chapter, let us take into deep consideration the events at Mount Sinai during the giving of the Ten Commandments which represent a profound moment of transformation and resurrection for the people of Israel. According to the Talmud, this occasion was not merely a historical event but a spiritual renewal that signified death and resurrection, linking deeply with the concept of the restoration of the pattern of Adam through the agency of the Word of YaH, the Torah.

The Talmud in Shabbat 88b provides a fascinating narrative about the experience of the Israelites at Mount Sinai. It describes how the people of Israel died and were resurrected during the revelation of the Ten Commandments:

"Rabbi Joshua ben Levi also said: When Moses ascended on high, the ministering angels spoke before the Holy One, Blessed be He: 'Sovereign of the Universe! What business has one born of woman among us?' He said to them: 'He has come to receive the Torah.' They said to Him: 'That secret treasure, which has been hidden by Thee for nine hundred and seventy-four generations before the world was created, You desire to give to flesh and blood!"...The Holy One, Blessed be He, said to Moses: 'Hold on to My Throne of Esteem and answer them!'"

This passage alludes to the immense spiritual significance of the Torah and the divine encounter. The Israelites experienced a form of spiritual death due to the overwhelming holiness and intensity of the divine revelation. However, they were revived by a miraculous divine intervention using the "dew of resurrection," as mentioned in Talmud Shabbat 88b:

"Rabbi Yehoshua ben Levi said: When the Israelites heard the utterance of the Ten Commandments from the mouth of the Holy One, Blessed be He, their souls departed, as it is stated: 'My soul went out when He spoke' (Song of Songs 5:6). *But since their souls departed at each commandment, how did they receive the second commandment? He brought down the dew with which He will revive the dead in the future and revived them."*

This "dew" symbolizes the divine life force and energy that revives and restores, hinting at the future resurrection and ultimate redemption. Connecting this event to the broader theme of the pattern of Adam, we understand that Adam was created as the archetype of humanity, endowed with the divine image and likeness. When Adam fell, humanity lost its direct connection to this divine archetype. However, through the giving of the Torah, Israel was given an opportunity to reclaim this divine pattern.

The Torah, referred to as the "Word of YaH," serves as the means through which this restoration and resurrection occur. The Word is seen as the divine blueprint for creation, and adherence to the Torah allows humanity to realign with its original divine purpose.

The concept of resurrection through the Word is not only a Talmudic idea but also deeply embedded in the Messianic Scriptures. In John 1:1-4, it is written:

"*In the beginning was the Word, and the Word was with Elohim, and the Word was Elohim. He was with Elohim in the beginning. Through him all things were made; without him nothing was made that has been made. In him was life, and that life was the light of all mankind.*"

This passage emphasizes the creative and life-giving power of the Word, paralleling the Talmudic idea of the divine dew that revives the dead. The Word, or Davar[32], is identified with Yeshua, who embodies the divine Word and brings life and resurrection to humanity. As such, Yeshua is the Torah made flesh (John 1.14), a reality which we all are to incarnate.

The Torah is thus seen as the medium through which the divine life is imparted to humanity. By receiving the Torah, Israel was not only given laws but was also infused with the Torah's life force that could restore them to the pattern of Adam. This is echoed in Deuteronomy 30:19-20:

"*This day I call the heavens and the earth as witnesses against you that I have set before you life and death, blessings and curses. Now choose life, so that you and your children may live and that you may love YaH your Elohim listen to his voice and hold fast to him. For YaH is your life, and he will give you many years in the land he swore to give to your fathers, Abraham, Isaac and Jacob.*"

Choosing life through obedience to the Torah aligns humanity with creation's original pattern and facilitates the restoration of the divine image on Earth through our agency as representatives of YaH on Earth. With the narrative of Israel's death and resurrection at Mount Sinai as recorded in the scroll of Exodus, we are provided a profound illustration of the transformative power of the Torah. This event foreshadows the ultimate resurrection and redemption that is central to both Rabbinic and Messianic thought. By engaging with the Word of YaH and living according to the principles of the Torah, humanity can reclaim the primordial pattern of Adam, once again embodying the image and likeness of Elohim. In this light, the Torah is not merely a set of rules but a divine gift that enables spiritual rebirth and alignment with the divine purpose for any and all who engage its principles. As we explore the depths of these teachings, we gain a deeper appreciation for the calling, responsibility and privilege of embodying the divine image, walking in the light of the Word and contributing to the ultimate redemption and restoration of creation. Therefore, let us be true to our Elohim, true to our cause and true to ourselves on this journey from life to life.

CHAPTER V
ALIGNING WITH THE PATTERN

As I'm personally arriving closer to the goal of becoming one with YaH, I'm realizing more and more that living in accordance with the pattern of Adam is not merely about understanding an ancient archetype; it's more so about embodying and activating the principles of faithfulness to the covenant, fulfillment of the commandments, doing deeds worthy of repentance, making atonement for trespasses and exhibiting righteous conduct as instructed by the Torah and Messianic Scriptures. With my life intent on adhering to Torah based teachings and traditions of our Israelite forebearers, it's my aim to explore what it means to align our lives with this heavenly revealed pattern from a Torah-based, Messianic perspective. I pray that the conveyance of the message I've been given to share with you is clear and able to be comprehended.

The cornerstone of living in the pattern of Adam is to have an unwavering faithfulness to YaH as our King. Being created in the image and likeness of Elohim, given rulership over creation and all life in it and tasked with being fruitful and multipliers of life, humanity's ability to accomplish all of these duties is based on being one with YaH.

We find this principle articulated in the Shema prayer, which is recited twice daily. The Shema encapsulates this principle with the words: "*Hear, O Israel: YaH is our Elohim, YaH is one. Love YaH your Elohim with all your heart and with all your soul and with all your strength*" (Deuteronomy 6:4-5). To align with the will of YaH is to align with the pattern of Adam which requires us to exercised absolute fidelity in covenant with YaH, ourselves and one another.

Thus faithfulness to YaH requires absolute devotion and an intimate, personal relationship with Him consequently leading to collective, or more specifically, Messianic consciousness. It is through this relationship that we find our true identity and purpose, enabling us to walk with Elohim just as Enoch was described as doing in Genesis 5.

As our faithfulness is expressed through guarding the covenant that YaH established with our ancestors, it should be clear to us that this covenant is both a privilege and a responsibility; a blessing and an undertaking. In Genesis 17:9, Elohim said to Abraham, "*As for you, you must keep my covenant, you and your descendants after you for the generations to come*." Guarding the covenant involves living by the statutes and commandments given to us by our teacher Moses and our Master Yeshua, ensuring that our lives reflect the holiness and justice of YaH.

Central to guarding the covenant is our fulfillment of the commandments, in Hebrew called mitzvot. As the Torah and Talmud provides detailed instructions on how to live a life that is pleasing to Elohim, it is our duty to praise the Master of all creation by the demonstration of our conduct in alignment with the will of YaH.

In Deuteronomy 30:16, it is written, "*For I command you today to love YaH your Elohim, to walk in obedience to him, and to keep his commands, decrees, and laws; then you will live and increase and YaH your Elohim will bless you in the land you are entering to possess.*" The fulfillment of the commandments brings blessings and aligns us with the divine order established at creation.

Despite the perfection in design of creation, humanity[33] and the natural order of existence, we all know that humanity is prone to error as some of our own poor decisions well prove. With the pattern of Adam, however, we are afforded the principle of teshuvah, or repentance, for the correction, or rectification, of our negative thought processes, emotionally inspired word choice and impulsive conduct.

As one of the seven things created before the first day, we are told about teshuvah in Pirkei DeRabbi Eliezer 3:3 that, "*Seven things were created before the world was created. They are: The Torah, Gehinnom [the lake of fire], the Garden of Eden, the Throne of Esteem, the Temple, Repentance and the Name of the Messiah.*"

As a primordial principle etched into the very fabric of creation, the significance of repentance is crucial in reestablishing the order of existence given the often impetuous nature of humanity and its inclination to stray from the paths of righteousness into transgression and error.

When we fall short of YaH's commandments, we are called to return to Him with sincere repentance when made aware of our misstep. The prophet Joel exhorts us, "*Return to YaH your Elohim, for he is kind and compassionate, slow to anger and abounding in love, and he relents from sending calamity*" (Joel 2:13). Repentance restores our relationship with YaH and realigns us with His will and the order of creation.

It should also be known that repentance is closely linked with atonement, a theme central to both the Torah and Messianic Scriptures. The Day of Atonement (Yom Kippur) is the pinnacle and holiest day of the year in Israelite culture, as outlined in Leviticus 16. This is a day when the holiest man on Earth, the high priest, goes into the holiest place on Earth, the Holy of Holies in the Jerusalem Temple, to make atonement for the holiest people on Earth, the kingdom of Israel, on the holiest day of the year, which again is Yom Kippur.

In the Messianic understanding, however, Yeshua is seen as the ultimate atonement for sin. In 1 John 2:2, it states, "*He is the atoning sacrifice for our sins, and not only for ours but also for the sins of the whole world.*" This prophetic revelation emphasizes that through Yeshua, our sins are forgiven, and we are reconciled with Elohim unto faithful obedience and righteousness.

This dynamic of the fulfillment of atonement is corroborated with a tractate from both the Jerusalem and Babylonian Talmud which speaks to a historical event taking place at the Temple addressing a fundamental transition in the method of achieving atonement following the death, burial and resurrection of Yeshua in the year 30 CE.

According to tradition it is written that "*Forty years before the destruction of the Temple,*" says the Jerusalem Talmud, "*the western light went out, the crimson thread remained crimson, and the lot for the Lord always came up in the left hand. They would close the gates of the Temple by night and get up in the morning and find them wide open*" (The Yerushalmi, translated by Jacob Neusner, p.156f).

It is recorded similarly in the Babylonian Talmud, "*Our Rabbis taught: During the last forty years before the destruction of the Temple the lot ['for the Lord'] did not come up in the right hand; nor did the crimson-colored strap become white; nor did the western-most light shine; and the doors of the HEKAL (TEMPLE) would open by themselves*' (The Soncino Talmud, tractate 'Yoma,' 39b)."[34]

That the death and resurrection of Yeshua ben Yoseph dramatically altered the way that atonement was effectuated for Israel becomes glaringly apparent in light of the prophecy of Daniel 9.24-27 where he is shown that, "*Seventy weeks are decreed for your people and for your set-apart city, to put an end to the transgression, and to seal up sins, and to cover crookedness, and to bring in everlasting righteousness, and to seal up vision and prophet, and to anoint the Most Set-apart. Know, then, and understand from the going forth of the command to restore and build Yerushalayim until Messiah the Prince is seven weeks and sixty-two weeks. It shall be built again, with streets and a trench, but in times of affliction. And after the sixty-two weeks Messiah shall be cut off and have naught. And the people of a coming prince shall destroy the city and the set-apart place. And the end of it is with a flood. And wastes are decreed and fighting until the end. And he shall confirm a covenant with many for one week. And in the middle of the week, he shall put an end to slaughtering and meal offering. And on the wing of abominations he shall lay waste, even until the complete end and that which is decreed is poured out on the one who lays waste.*"

Confirming both the time period of the appearance of the Messiah on Earth and the destruction of the Temple by the Roman Empire, this prophecy narrows the timeline and actually pinpoints the season and signs for these paradigm shifting events to take place. The purpose of this prophetic event was nothing more than to inspire Israel, and ultimately humanity, to return to the original pattern and design of Adam with which humanity was created to live in alignment with the will of YaH.

It is with this in mind that it should now be evident that living in accordance with the pattern of Adam involves being a vessel through which the presence of YaH is established on Earth. This is accomplished through our witness and righteous conduct. In Exodus 19:6, Elohim calls Israel to be "*a kingdom of priests and a holy nation*." Our role is to reflect YaH's holiness to the world through our actions. Yeshua echoes this in Matthew 5:14-16, saying, "*You are the light of the world. A town built on a hill cannot be hidden...let your light shine before others, that they may see your good deeds and give honor to your Father in heaven*."

The essence of living in the pattern of Adam is encapsulated in the principles of love in Spirit and Truth. This love is not just an emotion but a profound commitment to YaH and humanity; it is a selfless offering of oneself for the sake of demonstrating that the whole is greater than the part. Yeshua teaches, "*Love YaH your Elohim with all your heart and with all your soul and with all your mind. This is the first and greatest commandment. And the second is like it: Love your neighbor as yourself*" (Matthew 22:37-39). True love fulfills the Torah, as Sha'ul writes in Romans 13:10, "*Love does no harm to a neighbor. Therefore love is the fulfillment of the law.*"

Faithfulness to YaH: A Deeper Understanding

Living in accordance with the pattern of Adam is a holistic approach that encompasses devotional acts such as exercising faithfulness to YaH, guarding the covenant, fulfilling the commandments, undergoing repentance when missing the mark, accomplishing atonement, offering forgiveness, establishing YaH's presence on Earth and embodying love in Spirit and Truth. It is through these principles that we align ourselves with the divine purpose, truly reflecting the image and likeness of Elohim. As we delve deeper into the pages of this chapter, we will explore how these principles can transform our lives and the world around us, fulfilling the divine mandate given to Adam, codified by Moses and revealed through the Torah and the teachings of Yeshua.

Faithfulness to YaH is foundational to living in accordance with the pattern of Adam. Faithfulness is about a deep, unwavering commitment to the Most High, manifested by trust, obedience and devotion; offering ourselves as living offerings to YaH. At its heights, faithfulness is both a relational and a practical reality, influencing every aspect of our lives.

In the Hebrew Scriptures we repeatedly encounter the call for faithfulness to YaH. In Deuteronomy 7:9, we read:

"*Know therefore that YaH your Elohim is the Most High; He is the faithful El, keeping His covenant of love to a thousand generations of those who love Him and keep His commandments.*"

This verse brings to light the reciprocal nature of faithfulness: because YaH is faithful to His covenant, we in return are called to be faithful by loving YaH and keeping the commandments of the Torah. One of the most powerful examples of this in Scripture is the story of Abraham. Genesis 15:6 states:

"*Abram believed YaH, and He credited it to him as righteousness.*"

It was Abraham's determined trust in YaH's promises, despite seemingly impossible circumstances, that inspired him to walk in alignment with the will of YaH, subjecting his desires to that of the One who called and justified him. Abraham's life, as a result, serves as a remarkable paradigm of faith, or in Hebrew what is known as *emunah*[35]. This is the reason we call Abraham the "father of faith."

Taking an initial consideration of the Hebrew word *emunah,* a powerful principle emerges from the depths of meaning, providing us with insight into effective practices involved with exercising faith. One of the concepts that captures how to move in faith, as denoted by the meaning of the word emunah, is that of training. We find this particular expression of the principle explained allegorically by Rabbi Sha'ul in 1 Corinthians 9.24-27,

"Do you not know that those who run in a race indeed all run, but one receives the prize? Run in such a way as to obtain it. And

everyone who competes controls himself in every way. Now they do it to receive a corruptible crown, but we for an incorruptible crown. Therefore I run accordingly, not with uncertainty. Thus I fight, not as one who beats the air. But I treat my body severely and make it my slave, so that when I have proclaimed to others, I myself might be rejected."

From this passage it's clear that the Messianic Scriptures continue to emphasize the training aspect of faithfulness. Using the metaphor of athletic competition to illustrate the disciplined, rigorous nature of faith, this passage emphasizes the necessity of self-control, focus and dedication in the disciple's spiritual journey. With this in mind, let's delve into the essence of this verse relative to the connotation of faith as training.

Rav Sha'ul starts by comparing the life of faithfulness to that of a race. All believers are running, but the emphasis is on running with the intention of winning. This implies purpose and determination. Faith is not a passive state but an active pursuit of a goal – the prize of eternal life and union with Elohim. Just as athletes train rigorously to win a race, disciples must also commit to spiritual disciplines with the same intensity and focus.

Sha'ul goes on to highlight the importance of self-control, a key aspect of faith. Athletes exercise strict discipline over their bodies, diet and routines to achieve peak performance. Similarly, disciples must practice self-control in their spiritual lives. This involves resisting temptations, making sacrifices and staying committed to spiritual practices such as prayer, fasting and studying Scripture. The goal for disciples is far greater than a temporary, earthly reward; it is the eternal, incorruptible crown of life promised by YaH.

Sha'ul then emphasizes running with certainty and fighting with purpose. This signifies living a life of faith with clear intent and focus. Disciples are to pursue their spiritual goals with clarity and direction, avoiding aimless actions that have no eternal value. This intentionality reflects a deep understanding of one's purpose and mission in life, aligning daily actions with the ultimate goal of honoring YaH and advancing His kingdom.

Sha'ul concludes this instruction by stressing the importance of training and discipline. He likens his spiritual discipline to an athlete's rigorous training regimen, highlighting the necessity of making the body a servant to the spirit. This involves subjugating physical desires and impulses to ensure they do not hinder spiritual growth. By doing so, Paul ensures that his preaching is authentic and that he does not fall short of the very standards he teaches. This underscores the principle of leading by example and maintaining personal integrity. This is the essence of faith and what emunah explicitly prescribes for the disciple to undertake.

Taking another step deeper into the waters of faith, it is clear from the Hebrew context of the word emunah (אֱמוּנָה) that faith conveys a sense of steadfastness, truthfulness, veracity, trust, fidelity and unwavering commitment. It is derived from the root word *aman* (אָמַן), meaning to be firm, established and reliable.

For activation, faith involves more than just a verbal profession based on a conviction or belief; it requires action, training, confirmation, consistency and dedication. As we reflect on this principle, we are able to hear the whispers of the deeper meanings of emunah, emphasizing that faith is an active, committed relationship with YaH that requires steadfastness, dedication and continuous effort, not just intellectual acknowledgement. As disciples come to embody these principles, they reflect the image and likeness of Elohim, pursuing the eternal prize that unwavering devotion endows one with.

To expand on this point, the 11th chapter of Hebrews focuses on the faithfulness of many biblical figures. It is the first verse, however, that provides us with the operative principle of the entire chapter:

"*Faith is the substance of what is expected and the evidence of what is not seen*" (Hebrews 11:1).

From this verse two words emerge beside faith that brings a most powerful focus to light – substantial evidence. Though not as definitive as the principle *beyond a shadow of a doubt*, in the legal world substantial evidence *"refers to evidence that a reasonable mind could accept as adequate to support a conclusion*[36]*."*

Moreover, Yeshua teaches about the importance of faithfulness. In Matthew 7.24-25, He says "*Therefore everyone who hears these words of Mine, and does them, shall be like a wise man who built his house on the rock, and the rain came down, and the floods came, and the winds blew and beat on that house, and it did not fall, for it was founded on the rock.*"

This parable of the building a house illustrates that faithfulness is rewarded when enduring trials, something that would result from training and discipline in order to endure and overcome hardship and trials for the sake of the Kingdom.

Pirkei Avot 1:2 also speaks to the concept of faithfulness. In the oral tradition, Shimon the Righteous says:

"*The world stands on three things: on the Torah, on the service of Elohim and on acts of loving-kindness.*"

From this standpoint, faithfulness encompasses adherence to the Torah, service to Elohim and loving-kindness, which align with the holistic nature of faith, or emunah. Given the instructions of the Torah, it is when takes them to heart and engages in the service that Torah entails, it is then done with loving-kindness which is the demonstration of the matters of faith typical of someone who is in covenant with YaH.

That the Hebrew word for faith, emunah (אֱמוּנָה), is a matter of true apprehension of reality is discussed in depth by Maimonides in the 50th chapter of the Guide for the Perplexed[37]. Taking another step deeper into the waters of faith, we shall take another approach by examining each Hebrew letter that spells out the word, where we gain an even more profound understanding of what it means to be faithful to YaH.

- **Aleph** (א): Aleph represents the oneness, the primacy, the supremacy, the originality and ultimately the sovereignty of Elohim. It is understood as the primal cause and invisible force which reminds us that true faith begins with acknowledging YaH as the One True Elohim. From this standpoint, aleph suggestions Adam in perfect unity with the will of Elohim.

- **Mem** (מ): Denoting the idea of reflection, the letter mem symbolizes water, representing the flow and continuity of life. It suggests that the love of Elohim flows forth like water desiring to fill Adam and that faithfulness requires a continual, dynamic and fluid relationship with Elohim.

- **Vav** (ו): Perceived as the letter that unites all elements, from the highest to the lowest, vav is a connector, symbolizing that faith binds us to Elohim, His commandments and the Kingdom. As such, the vav serves as the point of connection that unites heaven and earth, giving Adam access to the Light of Truth that YaH has set aside for those who are faithful.

- **Nun** (נ): Nun signifies humility and faithfulness. It teaches us that faith requires a humble acknowledgment of our dependence on Elohim. In its fullest expression, nun represents the state of the world after rectification which leads to the Kingdom of Heaven established on Earth.

- **Hei** (ה): Hei represents revelation and divine breath. It underscores that faith is inspired by YaH's revelation and sustained by His spirit. In its fullest expression, hei takes on the meaning of the ultimate revelation of Messianic Consciousness[38].

Together, these letters paint a picture of emunah as a profound, active trust in YaH that influences every aspect of our being. Combining the meaning, we are arrive at this deeper innerstanding of faith: *Adam attains perfect unity with the will of YaH by reciprocating the flowing love of Elohim which connects to the Light of Truth that rectifies the soul for the ultimate revelation of Messianic Consciousness to be made manifest in the Kingdom.*

When we put our faith into action, it becomes clear that the objective is produce nothing short of the image and likeness of Elohim on Earth as it is in Heaven. This reality is made possible through the acquisition, acceptance of and alignment with the will of YaH. To experience this is to know that coming to that point involves a process that must be undertaken meticulously step by step along the journey. As to the steps taken to manifest the substantial evidence of faith, consider the following:

1. *Trust in YaH's Sovereignty*: Just as Abraham trusted in YaH's promises, we are called to trust in YaH's plans and timing, even when they are not immediately apparent.

2. *Obedience to the Commandments*: Faithfulness is demonstrated through obedience to YaH's laws, as outlined in the Torah. This includes both ritual observances and ethical conduct.

3. *Service and Worship*: Regular worship and service to YaH are expressions of our faithfulness. This includes prayer, study, and participation in communal worship.

4. *Acts of Loving-kindness*: Faithfulness is also shown in how we treat others. Acts of kindness, charity, and justice are integral to living out our faith.

5. *Repentance and Atonement*: When we fall short, faithfulness involves sincere repentance and seeking atonement. This restores our relationship with YaH and aligns us back with His will.

6. *Witness and Testimony*: Our lives should be a testimony of Elohim's faithfulness. By living out our faith, we bear witness to YaH's goodness and draw others to Him.

Faithfulness to YaH is the bedrock of living in accordance with the pattern of Adam. It is about a holistic commitment that encompasses trust, obedience, service, humility, and love. By embodying these principles, we fulfill our divine calling and reflect the image of Elohim in the world. As we delve deeper into this chapter, we will explore how these aspects of faithfulness can transform our lives and enable us to walk in the fullness of the pattern of Adam.

The concept of manifesting the image and likeness of Elohim is essential to our understanding of human purpose and potential. This divine blueprint calls us to reflect YaH's character in every aspect of our lives, both individually and collectively. To achieve this, we must engage in a holistic process that encompasses spiritual, emotional, mental, and physical dimensions. This section explores practical steps for manifesting the image and likeness of Elohim, integrating insights from the Hebrew and Messianic Scriptures, metaphysical spirituality, and scientific studies on consciousness. We will now consider more practical steps to take, both personally and collectively, to go about manifesting the image and likeness of Elohim on Earth.

PERSONAL APPLICATIONS

1. **Deepening Spiritual Practices**

To manifest the divine image, we must cultivate a deep, personal relationship with Elohim through consistent spiritual practices. This includes prayer, meditation, and the study of sacred texts.

- *Prayer and Meditation*: Engaging in regular prayer and meditation helps us align our thoughts and actions with YaH's will. Psalm 1:2 emphasizes the importance of meditating on YaH's Torah: "*But his delight is in the Torah of YaH, and on his Torah he meditates day and night.*" In regard to prayer, we are told by rabbi Sha'ul to "*pray without ceasing*" (1 Thessalonians 5.17).

- *Study of Scripture*: Immersing ourselves in the Scriptures provides guidance and insight into YaH's character and expectations. Joshua 1:8 instructs: "*Keep this Book of the Torah always on your lips; meditate on it day and night, so that you may be careful to do everything written in it. Then you will be prosperous and successful.*"

2. **Practicing Righteousness and Justice**

Manifesting the image of Elohim involves embodying His attributes of righteousness and justice in our daily lives.

- *Acts of Kindness and Charity*: Proverbs 21:3 states, "*To do righteousness and justice is more acceptable to YaH than sacrifice.*" Engaging in acts of kindness and charity reflects YaH's compassion and justice.

- *Integrity and Honesty*: Living with integrity and honesty is essential. Proverbs 11:3 teaches, "*The integrity of the upright guides them, but the unfaithful are destroyed by their duplicity.*"

3. **Cultivating Emotional and Mental Well-being**

Our emotional and mental states significantly impact our ability to reflect YaH's image. Practicing self-awareness, emotional regulation, and positive thinking can help align our inner lives with divine principles. We are given a glimpse into the significance of emotional stability and the power of reason over emotions as demonstrated by the apocryphal book 4 Maccabees 1:15-19 which informs us:

"*Now reason is the mind that with sound logic prefers the life of wisdom. Wisdom, next, is the knowledge of divine and human matters and the causes of these. This, in turn, is education in the Torah, by which we learn divine matters reverently and human affairs to our advantage. Now the kinds of wisdom are rational judgment, justice, courage and self-control. Rational judgment is supreme over all of these, since by means of it reason rules over the emotions.*"

To paint a clearer picture of how to gain authority over the emotions, consider being intentional and in control over these four areas of our personal well-being:

- Mindfulness and Self-Awareness: Developing mindfulness and self-awareness allows us to recognize and address negative emotions and thoughts. Philippians 4:8 encourages us to focus on positive qualities: "*Finally, brothers and sisters, whatever is true, whatever is noble, whatever is right, whatever is pure, whatever is lovely, whatever is admirable—if anything is excellent or praiseworthy—think about such things.*"

- Forgiveness and Healing: Embracing forgiveness and seeking emotional healing frees us from past hurts and allows us to experience YaH's peace. Colossians 3:13 instructs, "*Bear with each other and forgive one another if any of you has a grievance against someone. Forgive as YaH forgave you.*"

The following dynamics are suggested exercises and part of the collective application to bring about communal well-being:

Collective Applications

1. **Building Loving and Just Communities**

Manifesting the divine image collectively involves creating communities that embody YaH's love, justice and compassion.

- Community Service and Advocacy: Engaging in community service and advocacy for justice aligns our communities with YaH's heart for the oppressed. Isaiah 1:17 calls us to action: "*Learn to do right; seek justice. Defend the oppressed. Take up the cause of the fatherless; plead the case of the widow.*"

- Fostering Unity and Peace: Promoting unity and peace within our communities reflects YaH's desire for harmony. Ephesians 4:3 urges us to "*Make every effort to keep the unity of the Spirit through the bond of peace.*" This dynamic is also emphasized in Romans 12.16-18 where we exhorted to do the following: "*Be of the same mind toward one another. Do not be proud in mind but go along with the lowly. Do not be wise in your own estimation. Repay no one evil for evil. Respect what is right in the sight of all men. If possible, on your part, be at peace with all men.*"

2. **Encouraging Collective Spiritual Growth**

Encouraging collective spiritual growth through communal worship, study, and support helps reinforce heavenly principles in our communities.

- *Communal Worship and Study*: Gathering for communal worship and study strengthens our collective faith. Hebrews 10:24-25 advises, "*And let us consider how we may spur one another on toward love and good deeds, not forsaking the fellowship, as some are in the habit of doing, but encouraging one another—and all the more as you see the Day approaching.*"

- *Support and Accountability*: Providing support and accountability within our communities helps us stay committed to our spiritual goals. Galatians 6:2 emphasizes, "*Carry each other's burdens, and in this way you will fulfill the law of Messiah.*"

Metaphysical and Scientific Perspectives

As a philosophy minor, one of my favorite areas of study is that of metaphysics. Though introduced to the discipline during my collegiate years from Hellenist thought according to the schools of Socrates and Plato, it is the system of rabbi Moshe ben Maimon, aka Maimonides, with which I most resonate. As an area of science that he considered to be both essential and perilous, it is a field of study that yields the most effective result of coming to know and understand the secrets of Torah, or what Messiah Yeshua called the secrets of the Kingdom of the heavens[39].

With the word's origin, we find that "meta" means "beyond" and "physics" refers to the natural world. Metaphysics is a discipline that was known to Israelite priests and sages who utilized the field in order to deal with what lies beyond the physical sciences. Key areas of study within metaphysics include ontology (the study of being), cosmology (the study of the universe) and epistemology (the study of knowledge).

With metaphysics we find a science that explores the fundamental nature of reality, including the relationships between mind and matter, substance and attribute, potentiality and actuality. It seeks to answer the most profound questions about existence, reality, and the nature of things beyond the physical or empirical world. Central to metaphysics are concepts such as being, identity, time, space, causality and possibility.

1. **The Metaphysical Aspect of Spirituality**

Metaphysical spirituality explores the deeper, non-material aspects of our existence. It posits that we are interconnected with a divine source, and our spiritual practices can elevate our consciousness and align us with higher truths.

- *The Power of Intention and Thought*: Metaphysical teachings emphasize the power of intention and thought in shaping our reality. Proverbs 23:7 states, "*For as he thinks in his heart, so is he.*" This underscores the importance of cultivating positive and heavenly thoughts.

2. **Scientific Studies on Spiritual Consciousness**

Recent scientific studies have begun to quantify the impact of spiritual practices on consciousness and well-being.

- *Effects of Meditation and Prayer*: Research has shown that regular meditation and prayer can enhance brain function, reduce stress and improve overall individual and societal well-being. A study published in the journal "Frontiers in Psychology[40]" found that mindfulness meditation leads to changes in brain structure and function, improving emotional regulation and cognitive performance.

- *The Impact of Positive Emotions*: Studies on positive psychology demonstrate that cultivating emotions such as gratitude, love, and compassion can lead to better health outcomes and increased happiness. A study in the "Journal of Positive Psychology" found that practicing gratitude can enhance well-being and life satisfaction.

Manifesting the image and likeness of Elohim involves a comprehensive approach that integrates personal and collective spiritual practices, emotional and mental well-being, as well as active engagement in righteousness and justice. By deepening our relationship with YaH, practicing integrity and kindness, fostering community and embracing metaphysical insights and scientific findings, we can reflect YaH's character in our lives and contribute to the transformation of the world. This divine mandate calls us to live intentionally, align our actions with YaH's will and become beacons of light in a world in need of healing and restoration. As we strive to embody these principles, we fulfill our highest purpose and honor the divine image in which we were created.

QUANTUM PHYSICS AND SPIRITUALITY AS SACRED SCIENCE

Quantum physics, one of the most profound and revolutionary fields of modern science, delves into the fundamental nature of reality at the smallest scales. It examines the behavior of particles such as electrons and photons, revealing a world that operates far differently from the predictable, deterministic laws of classical physics. Central to quantum physics are concepts such as wave-particle duality, superposition, entanglement, and the observer effect, each of which challenges our conventional understanding of reality and opens up intriguing parallels with spiritual insights.

At its core, quantum physics studies the smallest components of the universe and their interactions. Unlike classical physics, which describes objects in precise terms, quantum mechanics operates in probabilities and uncertainties.

The intersection of quantum physics and spirituality invites us to view spiritual practices and experiences through the lens of scientific inquiry, treating spirituality as a form of sacred science. This approach bridges the gap between the material and the metaphysical, suggesting that the principles underlying quantum mechanics can enhance our understanding of spiritual consciousness.

Revisiting Hebrews 11:1, we come across what the author defines faith as "*the evidence of things not seen*" and "*the substance of things hoped for*." This description aligns remarkably with the principles of quantum physics, where unseen probabilities and potentialities form the foundation of observable reality.

- *Evidence of Things Not Seen*: In quantum mechanics, the behavior of particles is often inferred from indirect evidence rather than direct observation. Similarly, faith involves belief in realities and truths that are not immediately visible or tangible. However, by examining patters and types, our faith is bolstered by the principles that are present in such formations that allow disciples to arrive at logical and reasonable conclusions that make sense.

- *Substance of Things Hoped For*: Quantum physics posits that potential states (superpositions) exist as real possibilities until observed. Faith, in a parallel sense, regards hoped-for outcomes as having a substantive existence, influencing reality through belief and expectation.

Integrating quantum physics with spiritual consciousness enriches our understanding and practice of faith in several ways:

- *Interconnectedness and Oneness*: Quantum entanglement suggests a profound interconnectedness of all things, resonating with spiritual teachings about the unity of creation. This interconnectedness reinforces the spiritual principle of oneness with the divine and all living beings. As the Tabernacle in the Wilderness serves as a microcosm of the entire creation, we find this passage from Exodus 36.13 capturing the essence of interconnectedness and oneness of creation, creature and Creator: "*And he made fifty hooks of gold, and joined the curtains to each other with the hooks, and the Dwelling Place became one.*"

- *Role of the Observer*: The observer effect highlights the power of consciousness in shaping reality. This aligns with the idea that our beliefs, intentions, and prayers can influence outcomes, emphasizing the active role of faith in manifesting desired realities[40]. This principle is expressed in Psalm 34.8, where King David writes, "*Oh, taste and see that YaH is good; Blessed is the man that takes refuge in Him!*"

- *Embracing Uncertainty*: According to the Joint Quantum Institute, the "*uncertainty principle dictates that you cannot know the precise position and momentum of a particle at the same time, so the exact path it follows ends up being a little bit fuzzy, making the normal definitions of chaos and ergodicity challenging to apply*[41]." Quantum mechanics embraces uncertainty and ambiguity, encouraging a flexible and open-minded approach to spiritual growth. Faith, similarly, involves trust and surrender in the face of the unknown, fostering a deeper reliance on divine guidance. Proverbs 3.5-7 is the equivalent of flexible, open-mindedness in light of uncertainty, as it encourages us to "*trust in YaH with all your heart, And lean not on your own understanding; know Him in all your ways, and He makes all your paths straight. Do not be wise in your own eyes; fear YaH and turn away from evil.*"

SCIENTIFIC STUDIES ON SPIRITUAL CONSCIOUSNESS

Recent scientific studies have begun to explore and quantify the impact of spiritual practices on consciousness and well-being. Research in areas such as neurotheology and positive psychology demonstrates the measurable benefits of meditation, prayer, and mindfulness on brain function, emotional regulation, and overall health.

- *Neurotheology*: According to University of Tehran Department of Philosophy Professor Alireza Sayadmansour, neurotheology "also known as 'spiritual neuroscience', is an emerging field of study that seeks to understand the relationship between the brain science and religion. Scholars in this field, strive up front to explain the neurological ground for spiritual experiences such as "the perception that time, fear or self-consciousness have dissolved; spiritual awe; oneness with the universe." Studies in neurotheology examine how spiritual experiences affect the brain. Research using functional MRI scans shows that meditation and prayer can activate brain regions associated with compassion, empathy, and emotional stability[42].

- *Positive Psychology*: Research in positive psychology highlights the benefits of cultivating positive emotions such as gratitude, love, and compassion. These practices have been shown to enhance well-being, resilience, and life satisfaction.

Viewing spirituality through the lens of quantum physics and treating it as sacred science offers profound insights into the nature of faith and consciousness. By understanding the principles of interconnectedness, the observer effect and the embrace of uncertainty, we can deepen our practice of faith as described in Hebrews 11:1. This scientific approach to spiritual consciousness not only enhances our understanding of the unseen and hoped-for realities but also empowers us to actively participate in the co-creation of our spiritual and material worlds. As we bridge the realms of science and spirituality, we unlock new dimensions of human potential and divine connection, embodying the image and likeness of Elohim in ever more profound ways.

CHAPTER VI
THE MESSIANIC MISSION

In Exodus 19:5-6, we find a foundational passage that outlines the divine calling and mission of the people of Israel: "*Now therefore, if you will indeed obey my voice and keep my covenant, you shall be my treasured possession among all peoples, for all the earth is mine; and you shall be to me a kingdom of priests and a holy nation*." As we discussed this principle thoroughly in the Kingdom Within, this declaration by Elohim at Mount Sinai sets the stage for understanding Israel's unique role in the world and our covenant-based relationship with the El Shaddai.

The phrase "kingdom of priests" indicates that Israel is not merely a nation among nations, but one set apart with a priestly function. Priests in the Hebrew Bible are intermediaries between the Most High and humanity. They are consecrated to perform sacred rituals, offer sacrifices, and teach the divine laws. As Leviticus 10.10 tells us that the priesthood is "*to make a distinction between the set-apart and the profane, and between the unclean and the clean, and to teach the children of Yisra'ĕl all the laws which YaH has spoken to them by the hand of Mosheh*." This priestly role for Israel implies a collective responsibility to mediate YaH's presence, wisdom, and blessings to the rest of the world through delineating darkness from light and the implementation and application of a pedagogy based on the Torah.

Being a "holy nation" emphasizes the idea of sanctification and moral purity. The Hebrew word for holy (kadosh/,(קָדוֹשׁ means set apart or consecrated for a special purpose. Israel's calling involves living according to YaH's commandments, thereby reflecting His holiness and righteousness. This holiness is not just ritualistic but encompasses harnessed thoughts, selective speech, ethical behavior, pursuing justice and extending compassion as well.

We see this expressed in the following verses:

1. *Isaiah 61:6*: "*But you shall be called the priests of YaH; they shall speak of you as the ministers of our Elohim; you shall eat the wealth of the*

nations, and in their esteem you shall boast." This prophetic vision reinforces Israel's role as priests, serving YaH and being a conduit of His blessings to the nations.

2. 1 Peter 2:9: *"But you are a chosen race, a royal priesthood, a holy nation, a people for His own possession, that you may proclaim the excellencies of Him who called you out of darkness into His marvelous light."* This Messianic text echoes Exodus 19:5-6, extending the priestly and holy calling to the disciples of the Messiah, indicating the continuity of this divine mission through the Messianic community.

3. *Isaiah 49:6*: *"He says: 'It is too small a thing for you to be my servant to restore the tribes of Jacob and bring back those of Israel I have kept. I will also make you a light for the Gentiles, that my salvation may reach to the ends of the earth.'"* Here, the prophet Isaiah speaks of Israel's mission to be a light to the nations, highlighting the global scope of their calling.

Throughout history, Israel struggled to fully live out their calling as a kingdom of priests and a holy nation. Their failures led to exile and dispersion among the nations. However, YaH's plan for redemption and restoration remained steadfast. The coming of the Messiah is central to this redemptive narrative.

1. *Isaiah 53:5-6*: "B*ut he was pierced for our transgressions, he was crushed for our iniquities; the punishment that brought us peace was on him, and by his wounds we are healed. We all, like sheep, have gone astray, each of us has turned to our own way; and YaH has laid on him the iniquity of us all.*" This passage depicts the suffering servant, who takes upon himself the sins of Israel and the world, offering redemption and healing.

2. _Jeremiah 31:31-34_: "*The days are coming, declares YaH, when I will make a new covenant with the people of Israel and with the people of Judah. It will not be like the covenant I made with their ancestors when I took them by the hand to lead them out of Egypt, because they broke my covenant, though I was a husband to them, declares YaH. This is the covenant I will make with the people of Israel after that time, declares YaH. I will put my law in their minds and write it on their hearts. I will be their Elohim, and they will be my people.*" This prophetic promise of a new covenant speaks to the internalization of YaH's law, made possible through the Messiah.

3. _Romans 11:26-27_: "*And in this way all Israel will be saved. As it is written: 'The deliverer will come from Zion; he will turn godlessness away from Jacob. And this is my covenant with them when I take away their sins.'*" Paul emphasizes that the coming of the Messiah brings salvation to Israel, fulfilling YaH's covenant promises.

The Messiah's role is pivotal in restoring Israel to their divine calling. Through Yeshua, the promised Messiah, Israel is given the opportunity to renew their covenant relationship with Elohim. The Messiah's sacrificial death and resurrection open the way for spiritual renewal and transformation, enabling Israel to once again take up their priestly and holy mandate.

1. _John 1:29_: "The next day Yohanan saw Yeshua coming toward him and said, 'Look, the Lamb of Elohim, who takes away the sin of the world!'" Here, Yohanan the Baptist identifies Yeshua as the sacrificial Lamb, whose atoning death addresses the sin that separated Israel from their YaH-given mission.

2. _Hebrews 8:6_: "But in fact the ministry Yeshua has received is as superior to theirs as the covenant of which he is mediator is superior to the old one, since the new covenant is established on better promises." The author of Hebrews highlights the superiority of the new covenant mediated by Yeshua, which brings about the internalization of Elohim's laws and the transformation of hearts.

Our calling as Israel to be a kingdom of priests and a holy nation is a profound and enduring mandate, rooted in our covenant relationship with YaH. Despite our historical failures, the coming of the Messiah provided the means for restoration and the fulfillment of our divine mission. By living in accordance with the Torah and embodying the principles of faithfulness, obedience and love, we are empowered to reflect YaH's holiness and mediate His presence to the world. As disciples the Messiah, we are called to participate in this divine mission, striving to be a light in the darkness and agents of YaH's redemptive plan for humanity.

TORAH AS A PATH TO MESSIANIC TRANSFORMATION

The Torah is more than a set of laws and guidelines; it is a heavenly blueprint for living a life that is in harmony with YaH's will. As we delve deeper into its teachings, we uncover a path that leads to Messianic transformation—a journey toward spiritual maturity and alignment with the image and likeness of Elohim; a path to our perfection[44].

The Torah is often viewed as a path to holiness and righteousness. This is evident from various passages in the Hebrew Scriptures where adherence to the Torah is linked to life, prosperity and divine favor. Deuteronomy 30:15-16 states: "*See, I have set before you today life and good, death and evil. If you obey the commandments of YaH your Elohim that I command you today, by loving YaH your Elohim, by walking in His ways, and by keeping His commandments and His statutes and His rules, then you shall live and multiply, and YaH your Elohim will bless you in the land that you are entering to take possession of* it."

The Messianic transformation is thus rooted in obedience to the Torah, which serves as a guide for living in a way that is pleasing to YaH. This transformation is not merely external compliance but an internal change that aligns one's heart and mind with divine principles.

As we have discussed in the Kingdom Within, the word "Torah" itself means "instruction" or "teaching." It is intended to instruct YaH's people on how to live a life that reflects His character. Psalm 119:105 emphasizes this, stating: "*Your word is a lamp to my feet and a light to my path.*" The Torah illuminates the path to righteousness, providing wisdom and understanding that leads to a transformed life.

The Messianic Scriptures reinforces the transformative power of the Torah through the teachings of Yeshua and the apostles. Yeshua Himself stated in Matthew 5:17-18: "*Do not think that I have come to abolish the Torah or the Prophets; I have not come to abolish them but to fulfill them. For truly I say to you, until heaven and earth pass away, not a jot, not a tittle, will pass from the Torah until all is accomplished.*"

Yeshua's fulfillment of the Messianic prophecies for redemption Torah does not negate its importance but rather amplifies its intent. He embodied the Torah perfectly, demonstrating how its principles lead to a life that honors YaH. In this way, the Torah remains a crucial part of the Messianic transformation, guiding disciples towards a life that mirrors the Messiah.

The Mishnah provides further insights into the role of the Torah in personal and communal transformation. Pirkei Avot 6:6 lists 48 ways to acquire Torah, highlighting the comprehensive nature of Torah study and its impact on one's character and actions: "*The Torah is greater than the priesthood and the kingship, for the kingship is acquired through thirty qualifications, and the priesthood through twenty-four, while the Torah is acquired through forty-eight ways.*"

These ways include study, attentive listening, articulate speech, intuitive understanding, discernment, awe, reverence, humility, joy, purity, ministering to the sages, close association with colleagues, discussion with students, tranquility, study of the Scriptures, study of the Mishnah, limited business activity, limited engagement in worldly affairs, limited pleasure, limited sleep, limited conversation, limited laughter, patience, generosity, trust in the Sages, acceptance of suffering, knowing one's place, rejoicing in one's portion, placing a fence around one's words, claiming no credit for oneself, being beloved, loving Elohim, loving humanity, loving the ways of uprightness, loving justice, loving reproof, fleeing from honor, not being arrogant in learning, not taking pleasure in giving decisions, bearing the burden with one's fellow, judging him favorably, leading him to truth and peace, being composed in one's study, asking and answering, listening and contributing to the discussion, learning in order to teach and learning in order to practice.

Each of these practices reflects a methodical approach to acquiring the Torah, engaging the mind and spirit in a holistic learning process. As we brought to light in the previous chapter, recent studies in neuroscience, particularly in the field of neuroplasticity, demonstrate how sustained engagement in practices like meditation, study and ethical living can lead to significant changes in the brain. Neuroplasticity[45] refers to the brain's ability to reorganize itself by forming new neural connections throughout life. This scientific principle supports the idea that engaging deeply with the Torah and its teachings can transform one's mind and behavior, aligning with the spiritual renewal described in the scriptures. By understanding the overlap between these ancient practices and modern scientific discoveries, we gain a richer perspective on how the diligent study and application of the Torah can lead to profound personal and spiritual growth.

Romans 12:2 aligns with this scientific understanding: *"Do not be conformed to this world, but be transformed by the renewal of your mind, that by testing you may discern what is the will of Elohim, what is good and acceptable and perfect."* This renewal of the mind is a crucial aspect of the Messianic transformation, facilitated by the consistent study and application of Torah principles.

The Torah, by design, is a divine guide that leads to a life of holiness, righteousness and alignment with the will of YaH. Its principles, when studied and applied, bring about a profound transformation that reflects the image and likeness of Elohim. Through the teachings of Yeshua and the insights of the Mishnah, we see that the Torah's role in the Messianic transformation is integral and ongoing. As disciples engage deeply with these sacred texts, they experience a renewal of mind and spirit, embodying the divine attributes and fulfilling their calling as the children of light.

THE KEY TO TORAH FULFILLMENT

As we transition from understanding the transformative practices of acquiring the Torah to exploring its ultimate fulfillment, we delve into the profound insights offered at Romans 10:4. This passage states, "*For Messiah is the goal of the Torah unto righteousness to everyone who believes.*" To fully grasp the implications of this statement, we must unlock the deeper meanings embedded within the Torah and how they are fulfilled in the Messianic context.

First, however, we will consider the Greek word used in Romans 10:4 for "end," which is "telos;" this word can be translated as "goal" or "purpose." This implies that Messiah is the ultimate purpose or goal of the Torah; not just to come to Yeshua by faith, but to manifest within through faithfulness. From this perspective, rather than indicating the termination of the Torah, this verse points to the culmination and fulfillment of its teachings in the life and work of Yeshua.

Being that this principle applies to all of the disciples of the Messiah who find themselves rooted in Yeshua, let us heed what He shared with his taught ones at John 15.7-10, "*If you stay in Me and My Words stay in you, you shall ask whatever you wish and it shall be done for you. In this My Father is esteemed, that you bear much fruit, and you shall be My taught ones. As the Father has loved Me, I have also loved you. Stay in My love. If you guard My commands you shall stay in My love, even as I have guarded My Father's commands and stay in His love.*"

This verse captures a profound theological truth about the role of Yeshua in fulfilling the Torah and the transformative process that believers undergo as disciples of the Messiah. The concept of Yeshua being the Torah made flesh is rooted in the understanding that He embodies the perfect fulfillment of the Torah's commandments and principles. John 1:14 declares, "*The Word became flesh and made his dwelling among us. We have seen his esteem, the esteem of the one and only Son, who came from the Father, full of favor and truth.*" Here, "the Word" (Davar-Hebrew/Logos-Greek) is understood as the divine expression of YaH's will and wisdom, which in Israelite thought is intricately linked to the Torah.

To understand this concept, we look back to the Hebrew Scriptures, which provide a foundation for the Messianic fulfillment. As we've previously stated, in Deuteronomy 18:18-19, YaH promises to raise up a prophet like Moses: "*I will raise up for them a prophet like you from among their brothers. I will put my words in his mouth, and he will tell them everything I command him. I myself will call to account anyone who does not listen to my words that the prophet speaks in my name.*" This prophecy points to the coming of the Messiah, who would embody and expound upon the Torah, leading us back to our primordial nature.

Isaiah 42:1-4 also speaks of the servant of YaH, who will bring justice and be a light to the nations: "*Here is my servant, whom I uphold, My chosen one in whom I delight; I will put my Spirit on Him, and He will bring justice to the nations. He will not shout or cry out or raise His voice in the streets. A bruised reed He will not break, and a smoldering wick he will not snuff out. In faithfulness, He will bring forth justice; He will not falter or be discouraged till He establishes justice on earth. In His teaching, the islands will put their hope.*" This servant is seen as the Messiah, fulfilling the purpose of the Torah through his life and teachings.

Unlocking the key to Torah fulfillment involves recognizing the Torah as a living and dynamic guide that finds its ultimate expression in the Messiah. The Hebrew Scriptures and the teachings of Yeshua all point towards this fulfillment, emphasizing a life of love, righteousness and alignment with YaH's will. As we embody these principles, we participate in the transformative journey that the Torah invites us to undertake, leading to a deeper relationship with YaH and a more profound expression of our faith.

Yeshua's life, teachings, death, and resurrection are the ultimate realization of the Torah's intent and purpose. He lived a life of perfect obedience to YaH's commandments, thereby becoming the living embodiment of the Torah. His actions, teachings and sacrificial love demonstrated the heart of the Torah: love for YaH and love for neighbor (Matthew 22:37-40); something to which we are all called to accomplish.

As disciples of Yeshua, we are called to undergo a transformative process akin to Yeshua's own embodiment of the Torah. This process involves:

1. *Internalizing the Teachings of the Torah*: Just as Yeshua internalized the Torah and lived it out perfectly, we as disciples are called to write the Torah on our hearts (Jeremiah 31:33). This means allowing the principles of YaH's Word to shape our thoughts, actions and character.

2. *Living Out the Commandments*: Yeshua emphasized the importance of living out the commandments in their truest form. In the Sermon on the Mount (Matthew 5-7), He expounded on the deeper, spiritual implications of the Torah's commandments, calling His disciples to a higher standard of righteousness.

3. *Transformation Through the Spirit*: The indwelling of the Holy Spirit empowers disciples to live according to the Torah's principles. Paul speaks of this transformative power in Romans 8:4, saying, "*in order that the righteous requirement of the law might be fully met in us, who do not live according to the flesh but according to the Spirit.*" Selah.

4. *Reflecting YaH's Love and Holiness*: Just as Yeshua reflected YaH's love and holiness through His life, disciples are called to be holy as YaH is holy (1 Peter 1:15-16) and to love one another as He loved us (John 13:34).

The call to embody the Torah is rooted in the Shema prayer, where YaH commands Israel to love Him with all their heart, soul and strength, and to impress His commandments upon their hearts (Deuteronomy 6:4-9). Paul's writings also consistently urge believers to be transformed by the renewing of their minds (Romans 12:2) and to walk in the Spirit (Galatians 5:16). The Mishnah teaches the importance of study and practice of the Torah. Being that this blueprint is before us, the process to becoming Messianic and returning to the pattern of Adam that we were created to uphold, our process is, in fact, a simple one which requires discipline and dedication, a matter that is not, however, easy.

As we reflect on Romans 10:4, it should provide us with a revelation that Yeshua is the culmination of the Torah, embodying its principles and purpose in His life. It should also make us fully aware that as His disciples, we are called to undergo a similar transformation, internalizing the Torah, living out its commandments, and reflecting YaH's love and holiness. This process, empowered by the Holy Spirit, allows us to become living embodiments of the Torah, fulfilling our calling to be a kingdom of priests and a holy nation. Through this transformation, we align ourselves with the divine purpose, bringing the reality of YaH's Kingdom to earth.

CHAPTER VII
EMBRACING THE PATTERN

In this final chapter, we embark on a journey of return—a journey to our primordial nature as envisioned in the divine blueprint of the Torah. This return involves a deep, transformative process of repentance, spiritual discipline, and the overcoming of our baser, animal nature to ascend to our heavenly nature. Rabbi Sha'ul provides profound insight into this journey in 1 Corinthians 15:42-58, where he contrasts the first Adam with the last Adam, Yeshua the Messiah.

Sha'ul's epistle to the Corinthians lays the foundation for understanding the transformative journey from our earthly nature to our heavenly calling. He writes: "*So will it be with the resurrection of the dead. The body that is sown is perishable, it is raised imperishable; it is sown in dishonor, it is raised in honor; it is sown in weakness, it is raised in power; it is sown a natural body, it is raised a spiritual body. If there is a natural body, there is also a spiritual body. So it is written: 'The first man Adam became a living being'; the last Adam, a life-giving spirit. The spiritual did not come first, but the natural, and after that the spiritual. The first man was of the dust of the earth; the second man is of heaven*" (1 Corinthians 15:42-47).

Sha'ul's contrast between the two Adams highlights the journey from our fallen state to the redeemed state. The first Adam, created from the dust, symbolizes our natural, earthly existence prone to corruption and sin. In contrast, the last Adam, Yeshua, represents the life-giving spirit that restores and transcends our fallen nature.

As we have previously emphasized, repentance, or teshuvah in Hebrew, is the essential first step in our journey back to our primordial nature. It involves a heartfelt return to YaH, turning away from sin, and committing to a life aligned with His will in fulfillment of the commandments and keeping of the covenant. As the Prophet Isaiah exhorts, "*Seek YaH while he may be found; call on him while he is near. Let the wicked forsake their ways and the unrighteous their thoughts. Let them turn to YaH, and He will have mercy on them, and to our Elohim, for He will freely pardon*" (Isaiah 55:6-7).

Repentance is not merely an act of contrition but a profound transformation of the heart and mind, leading to a renewed relationship with Elohim. This renewal is necessary for overcoming our animal nature and reclaiming our identity as bearers of the divine image.

In his classic treatise, *Duties of the Heart*[46], by rabbi Bachya ibn Pekudah, he states, "*With regard to what is repentance, I say that repentance means that a man makes himself fit to resume the service of the Creator after he went out of it and transgressed against it, and to restore what he lost in it. This could be due to: ignorance of G-d and of the matters of serving Him, his evil inclination had overpowered his understanding, neglect of his duties towards G-d, associating with bad company who entice him to sin, or other similar reasons, as the wise man said: "My son, if sinners entice you, do not consent" (Proverbs 1:10), and "My son, fear YaH and the king; and meddle not with them that are given to change" (Proverbs 24:21).*

Spiritual Disciplines: Overcoming the Animal Nature

As has been presented with mounting evidence, the journey to transcend our earthly nature requires the cultivation of spiritual disciplines that align our lives with heavenly principles. As we draw near this works close, let us take yet another moment to revisit these vital spiritual disciplines for our ascent which include:

1. *Prayer and Meditation*: Regular prayer and meditation on YaH's Word draw us closer to Him, fostering a deeper spiritual connection and awareness. Yeshua exemplified this discipline, often retreating to solitary places to pray (Luke 5:16).

2. *Study of the Scriptures*: Immersing ourselves in the Torah and the teachings of Yeshua transforms our minds and hearts, guiding us in righteous living. As the Psalmist declares, "Your word is a lamp for my feet, a light on my path" (Psalm 119:105).

3. *Fasting and Self-Denial*: Fasting and other forms of self-denial help us master our physical desires and focus on spiritual growth. Yeshua taught the importance of fasting as a means of drawing closer to YaH (Matthew 6:16-18).

4. *Acts of Kindness and Charity*: Engaging in acts of kindness and charity reflects YaH's love and compassion to others, reinforcing our commitment to live out His commandments. As the prince of the Messianic community following the ascent of his brother Yeshua, James the Just writes, "*Religion that YaH our Father accepts as pure and faultless is this: to look after orphans and widows in their distress and to keep oneself from being polluted by the world*" (James 1:27).

5. *Community and Fellowship*: Participating in a community of believers provides support, accountability, and encouragement in our spiritual journey. The early disciples "*devoted themselves to the apostles' teaching and to fellowship, to the breaking of bread and to prayer*" (Acts 2:42).

With these disciplines in motion, we are able to undergo the process of transformation, renewing our entire being and the environment of which we are a part. Through devoted, dedicated and consistent effort, our lives will come to take on the primordial light that we are told is infused with every sentient matter in existence. It is time for us to assume our rightful position, once again, as the stars of the heavens, and shine our light so that the world knows that YaH lives, and we are His vessels.

It is in this spirit that Sha'ul concludes his discussion in 1 Corinthians 15 with a triumphant declaration of the ultimate transformation awaiting believers: "*Listen, I tell you a mystery: We will not all sleep, but we will all be changed—in a flash, in the twinkling of an eye, at the last trumpet. For the trumpet will sound, the dead will be raised imperishable, and we will be changed. For the perishable must clothe itself with the imperishable, and the mortal with immortality. When the perishable has been clothed with the imperishable, and the mortal with immortality, then the saying that is written will come true: 'Death has been swallowed up in victory'*" (1 Corinthians 15:51-54).

This promise of resurrection and transformation underscores the ultimate goal of our journey: to be conformed to the image of the last Adam, Yeshua, and to participate in His eternal kingdom. As we embrace the pattern of Adam revealed in the Torah and fulfilled in Yeshua, we move from mortality to immortality, from corruption to incorruption, and from earthly beings to heavenly citizens.

Our return journey to our primordial nature is a path of repentance, spiritual discipline, and transformation. By following the pattern of Adam as revealed in the Torah and embodied by Yeshua, we reclaim our identity as children of YaH, destined for esteem and immortality. Let us, therefore, commit ourselves to this journey with faith, perseverance, and love, striving to manifest the image and likeness of Elohim in our lives and bringing His kingdom to earth.

Grasping the Depth of Adam's Pattern

With this next section of our chapter, it is essential to take a moment to reflect on the journey we have embarked upon. This journey has taken us through the profound insights of Torah, the transformative power of repentance, and the spiritual disciplines required to transcend our earthly nature. In this section, we will simplify these concepts to ensure clarity and understanding, grounding our reflections in the enduring truths of Scripture.

The pattern of Adam, as we have explored, is a divine blueprint for humanity. It begins with the creation of Adam in Genesis 1:26-27, where Elohim says, "*Let us make man in our image, in our likeness, so that they may rule over the fish in the sea and the birds in the sky, over the livestock and all the wild animals, and over all the creatures that move along the ground*." This passage underscores our creation in the divine image, endowed with the purpose to reflect YaH's character and exercise stewardship over creation.

In the Messianic Scriptures, this pattern finds its ultimate fulfillment in Yeshua, who we just read about is described as the "last Adam" at 1 Corinthians 15:45. Yeshua embodies the perfect image of Elohim, living a life of complete obedience and love. As His disciples, we are called to follow His example and undergo a transformation that aligns us with this heavenly pattern. We are able to do so by exercising the following practices:

1. *Repentance and Renewal*: The journey begins with repentance, a heartfelt return to Elohim. As it is written in Isaiah 40.3-5, "*Prepare the way of YaH; make straight in the desert a highway for our Elohim. Let every valley be raised, and every mountain and hill made low. And the steep ground shall become level, and the rough places smooth. And the esteem of YaH shall be revealed, and all flesh together shall see it. For the mouth of YaH has spoken.*"

2. *Spiritual Disciplines*: To overcome our baser nature, we must engage in spiritual disciplines. Prayer, study of Scripture, fasting, acts of kindness, and community fellowship are essential practices. Yeshua emphasizes the importance of these practices in passages like Matthew 6:16-18 (fasting) and Acts 2:42 (community).

3. *Transformation and Resurrection*: The ultimate goal is our transformation from mortal beings to immortal, reflecting the likeness of Elohim. Recalling the Law of Equivalence of Form, based on the alignment of organism and environment, Paul's teaching in 1 Corinthians 15:51-54 assures us of this hope: "*For the trumpet will sound, the dead will be raised imperishable, and we will be changed.*"

Throughout the Scriptures, the themes of repentance, spiritual growth, and transformation are recurrent. In the Hebrew Bible, passages like Ezekiel 36:26-27 promise a new heart and spirit, symbolizing the inner transformation required to live out YaH's commandments: "*I will give you a new heart and put a new spirit in you; I will remove from you your heart of stone and give you a heart of flesh.*"

The Messianic Scripture echoes these themes, emphasizing the transformative power of the Spirit. Romans 12:2 encourages believers, "*Do not conform to the pattern of this world, but be transformed by the renewing of your mind. Then you will be able to test and approve what YaH's will is—his good, pleasing and perfect will.*"

By testing and approving the will of YaH in our lives, it will be easier for us to come to understand that Adam's pattern is not merely an intellectual exercise; it requires a heartfelt commitment to live according to YaH's design. It calls us to reflect on our daily lives, aligning our actions, thoughts and desires with the will of our Father and King. As we embrace repentance and spiritual disciplines, we participate in the transformative work of the Spirit, becoming more like Yeshua and fulfilling our role as bearers of YaH's image.

To grasp the depth of Adam's pattern, we must recognize that this journey is ongoing and dynamic. It involves constant self-reflection, growth and reliance on YaH's favor. The teachings of the Mishnah also remind us of the practical steps in this journey: "*Rabbi Jacob said: this world is like a vestibule before the world to come; prepare yourself in the vestibule, so that you may enter the banqueting-hall.*" (Pirkei Avot 4:16). This rabbinic wisdom reminds us that our time in this world is finite and serves as a preparation for the eternal life that we have been promised by Yah will come. By observing the commandments and living ethically, we prepare ourselves for the ultimate reward in the world to come, much like preparing in a vestibule before entering a grand banqueting hall.

As we continue to delve deeper into this sacred journey, let us hold fast to these principles, drawing strength from the Scriptures and the example of Yeshua. Our calling is to be transformed into His likeness, shining as children of light in a world in need of YaH's love and truth.

Empowered by Torah, Transformed by Messiah: Stepping into Messianic Destiny

Now armed with love and truth, the most powerful forces in creation, we embark on the journey of becoming who we are divinely called to be—reflectors of the image and likeness of Elohim.

The Torah, as the foundational guide for righteous living, coupled with the transformative power of the Messiah, equips us to embody our divine purpose. In this section, we explore the profound implications of being empowered by Torah and transformed by the Messiah, and how this dual empowerment leads us to fulfill our Messianic destiny.

To be empowered by Torah means to internalize its principles and allow them to shape our thoughts, actions, and character. Deuteronomy 6:6-7 commands, "*These words that I command you today shall be on your heart. You shall teach them diligently to your children...*" This passage emphasizes the importance of embedding Torah within our hearts, making it an intrinsic part of our daily lives. The Torah is not merely to be followed mechanically but to be internalized so that it transforms us from within.

Internalizing the Torah is what allows for us to now walk in the Light of YaH, affording us the ability to use discernment and make sound decisions based on the Word of Life. Psalm 119:105 declares, "*Your word is a lamp to my feet and a light to my path.*" It is clear from this verse that the commandments of Torah illuminate our way, guiding us in truth and righteousness. By living according to these divine instructions, we walk in the light, avoiding the pitfalls of darkness and sin.

Additionally, the Torah provides ethical standards that foster justice, compassion and humility. Deuteronomy 16.18-20 encapsulates this: "*Appoint judges and officers within all your gates, which YaH your Elohim is giving you, according to your tribes. And they shall judge the people with righteous right-ruling. Do not distort right-ruling. Do not show partiality, nor take a bribe, for a bribe blinds the eyes of the wise and twists the words of the righteous. Follow righteousness, righteousness alone, so that you live and inherit the land which YaH your Elohim is giving you.*"

Being that is the community's responsibility to establish order and peace in our dwellings, it is imperative that we follow the standard of righteousness and justice for our lives. As Yeshua comes to provide us with the exact representation and express image of Elohim for personal and collective action, we are able perceive the pattern as the Messiah not only fulfills the Torah but also brings a transformative power that renews and revitalizes us. Through Him, we gain the strength to live out the Torah's principles in a deeper and more profound way.

2 Corinthians 5:17 informs us that, "*...if anyone is in Messiah, he is a new creation. The old has passed away; behold, the new has come.*" This transformation signifies a rebirth, where our old sinful nature is replaced with a new nature aligned with YaH's sovereign will.

Not only are able to experience transformation, but also empowerment. For the purpose of bringing an age of peace into existence, Acts 1:8 promises, "*But you will receive power when the Holy Spirit has come upon you, and you will be my witnesses*..." The Holy Spirit empowers us to live out the Torah's commandments with favor and truth, enabling us to be effective witnesses of YaH's kingdom.

For it is through Yeshua's life and teachings which exemplify perfect obedience to Torah that shows us that it is possible to live a life that pleases YaH. For it is our Messianic destiny which involves living as a holy nation and a kingdom of priests, as outlined in Exodus 19:5-6. This calling requires us to embody the principles of Torah and the transformative power of the Messiah. And when we embody the attributes of YaH—love, justice, mercy and humility—we reflect His image. This divine mandate is fulfilled as we live out the principles of Torah and the teachings of Yeshua.

The purpose of this calling to live as a kingdom of priests, is to fulfill our role as mediator of YaH's presence to the world. 2 Corinthians 5.18-20 goes on to tell us that "*all matters are from Elohim, who has restored us to favor with Himself through Yeshua Messiah, and has given us the service of restoration to favor; that is, that Elohim was in Messiah restoring the world to favor unto Himself, not reckoning their trespasses to them, and has committed to us the word of restoration to favor. Therefore, we are envoys on behalf of Messiah, as though Elohim were pleading through us. We beg, on behalf of Messiah: Be restored to favor with Elohim.*"

As envoys, or emissaries on behalf of Messiah, we are folly invested with power to carry out the affairs of our King, representing the Kingdom with righteous conduct and power, demonstrating to the world that YaH Lives. For us, this means that living righteously involves more than adherence to laws; it is about embodying the Spirit of the Torah as Romans 8:4 explains that "the righteous requirement of the law might be fulfilled in us, who walk not according to the flesh but according to the Spirit."

Being empowered by Torah and transformed by the Messiah involves a holistic approach to life, where our actions, thoughts, and character align with Elohim's will. As we embrace this path, we fulfill our Messianic destiny, becoming true reflectors of the image and likeness of Elohim. This journey transforms us into vessels of YaH's love and truth, capable of bringing light to a world in need.

As we come to the close of this journey, let us remember the profound responsibility and privilege that lies before us. We are called to embrace the divine pattern revealed in the Torah and fulfilled in the Messiah. This call is not just to personal transformation but to actively participate in ushering in the Messianic Era, a time of peace, justice and the manifestation of Shekinah Presence of YaH on earth.

The scriptures are replete with calls to action, urging us to live out our faith in tangible ways. Isaiah 42:6-7 reminds us of our divine mandate: "*I, YaH, have called you in righteousness; I will take hold of your hand. I will keep you and will make you to be a covenant for the people and a light for the Gentiles, to open eyes that are blind, to free captives from prison and to release from the dungeon those who sit in darkness.*" This prophetic vision calls us to be active participants in YaH's redemptive work on Earth, bringing light to the nations in darkness, formlessness and void.

Similarly, the Great Commission given by Yeshua in Matthew 28:18-20 is a clarion call for all disciples: "*All authority in heaven and on earth has been given to me. Therefore, go and make disciples of all nations, baptizing them in the name of the Father and of the Son and of the Holy Spirit, and teaching them to obey everything I have commanded you. And surely I am with you always, to the very end of the age.*" This commission extends the call to bring the teachings and redemptive power of the Messiah to every corner of the earth, fulfilling the mission of Israel to be a light to the nations.

To fulfill the Great Commission, we must first truly embrace the attern of Adam and the divine image, integrating these key actions into our lives:

1. *Study and Teach the Torah*: Make a commitment to study the Torah and Messianic Scriptures regularly. As Deuteronomy 6:6-commands, teach these truths diligently to your children and to others. Knowledge of YaH's word is the foundation of living in His image.

2. _Live Righteously_: Emulate the character of Elohim by living out the ethical and moral teachings of the Torah. Micah 6:8 instructs us to "act justly, love mercy, and walk humbly with your Elohim." This is the essence of reflecting YaH's image.

3. _Engage in Community_: Actively participate in a community of faith where you can encourage and be encouraged. Ephesians 4:1-6 exhorts us to "...*to walk worthily of the calling with which you were called, with all humility and meekness, with patience, bearing with one another in love, being eager to guard the unity of the Spirit in the bond of peace – one body and one Spirit, as you also were called in one expectation of your calling, one Master, one belief, one immersion, one Elohim and Father of all, who is above all, and through all, and in you all.*"

4. _Practice Compassion and Justice_: In every interaction, seek to demonstrate the compassion and justice of Elohim. Proverbs 31:8-9 calls us to "*speak up for those who cannot speak for themselves, for the rights of all who are destitute. Speak up and judge fairly; defend the rights of the poor and needy.*"

5. _Proclaim the Good News_: Share the message of redemption through Yeshua the Messiah with others. Romans 10:14-15 underscores the importance of this mission: "*How, then, can they call on the one they have not believed in? And how can they believe in the one of whom they have not heard? And how can they hear without someone preaching to them? And how can anyone preach unless they are sent? As it is written: 'How beautiful are the feet of those who bring good news*!'"

The Messianic Era is not just a future hope but a present reality we are called to bring forth through our actions and faith. As we align our lives with the pattern of Adam and the image of Elohim, we become catalysts for the Kingdom of Heaven on earth.

Revelation 21:3-4 gives us a glimpse of this ultimate fulfillment: "And I heard a loud voice from the throne saying, 'Look! YaH's dwelling place is now among the people, and he will dwell with them. They will be his people, and YaH himself will be with them and be their Elohim. He will wipe every tear from their eyes. There will be no more death' or mourning or crying or pain, for the old order of things has passed away."

We are invited to participate in this divine narrative, to be agents of YaH's kingdom, bringing His light, love, and truth into every aspect of our world. By embracing this sacred call, we step into our true identity as children of light, reflecting the image and likeness of Elohim and preparing the way for the Messiah's return.

Let us then rise to this challenge with joy and determination, knowing that our efforts are part of a divine plan that transcends time and space. May we, through our faithfulness and obedience, hasten the coming of the Messianic Era and the restoration of all things.

"*Arise, shine, for your light has come, and the esteem of YaH rises upon you*" (Isaiah 60:1).

"*For we are YaH's handiwork, created in Messiah Yeshua to do good works, which YaH prepared in advance for us to do*" (Ephesians 2:10).

Let us embrace the pattern of Adam and fulfill our divine destiny of bringing creation back into its original design.

Amen, amen.

FOOTNOTES

1. Luke 17.20-21
2. [1] Taken from the idea of what is hidden is what is revealed/received, Kabbalah is comprehended to be the secret instruction of the Torah. Dictionary of Torah Names and Words. #6904-6905.
3. [1] "As man's distinction consists in a property which no other creature on earth possesses, viz., intellectual perception, in the exercise of which he does not employ his senses, nor move his hand or his foot, this perception has been compared--though only apparently, not in truth--to the Divine perception, which requires no corporeal organ. On this account, i.e., on account of the Divine intellect with which man has been endowed, he is said to have been made in the form and likeness of the Almighty, but far from it be the notion that the Supreme Being is corporeal, having a material form." Guide for the Perplexed. Moses ben Maimon. pg. 14
4. [1] *The Grand Unified Field Theory*, according to Encyclopedia Britannica, is the attempt to describe all fundamental forces and the relationships between elementary particles in terms of a single theoretical framework.
5. [1] *Pirke Avot* is a section from the Mishnah, or Oral Law, that contains short statements most often attributed to rabbis who lived around the beginning of the Common Era.
6. *[1] The Dictionary of Torah Names and Words* defines the Torah as *Law (Torah, תּוֹרָה); from the root "yarah/יָרָה " meaning "to teach, instruct, direct, cast, throw"; the teachings that renew the mind unto life; lit., the composite knowledge in all realms of light & life; universal administration of the knowledge, or Mind, of Light: from the four corners of the world, there is knowledge conducive unto life—universal knowledge or the logos of Light: the revelation of the full capacities of man, the measurement of man—[which is] The Messiah; a foundational testimony of the utter sufficiency of the Chief Cornerstone (Jn. 5:39), Torah—as Mashiyach/Messiah, the actualization of the Law— is spiritual: the spiritual base of being within every person (Rom. 7:14; 10:4; Jn. 3:6; Rev. 13:8; Jn. 4:20). Values, 605: the measurement of Messiah's life and Light; 611: the measurement of the activities of Principle. See statutes/ordinances.*
7. [1] John 14.6
8. [1] https://sacred-texts.com/jud/gfp/gfp003.htm
9. [1] Guide for the Perplexed; page 14
10. [1] Ibid. page 15
11. [1] Kabbalah is the transmission and reception of the secrets of the Torah. We read of this tradition in the Messianic Scriptures in

regard to Yahoshua's teachings which contained Kabbalistic overtones as he tells His disciples at Matthew 13.11, "Because it has been given to you to know the secrets of the Kingdom of Heaven, but to them it has not been given."

12. [1] According to the Jewish Encyclopedia, "Mishnah," the derivative of the verb "shanah," means...(1) "instruction," the teaching and learning of the tradition, the word being used in this sense in Ab. iii. 7, 8; and (2) in a concrete sense, the content of that instruction, the traditional doctrine as it was developed down to the beginning of the third century of the common era. "Mishnah" is frequently used, therefore, to designate the law which was transmitted orally, in contrast to "Miḳra," the law which is written and read (e.g., B. M. 33a; Ber. 5a; Ḥag. 14a; 'Er. 54b; Ḳid. 30a; Yer. Hor. iii. 48c; Pes. iv. 130d; Num. R. xiii.; and many other passages); and the term includes also the halakic midrashim (the expounding of Torah), as well as the Tosefta (the companion text of the Mishna) or explanatory additions to the Mishnah.

13. [1] According to the Jewish Encyclopedia, Pirkei Avot is "[t]he name of a small but highly valuable treatise of the Mishnah containing the oldest collection of ethical maxims and aphorisms of rabbinical sages. It is the last of the nine treatises belonging to Neziḳin [the order of damages relative to criminal and civil law is Israelite society], the fourth section of the Mishnah collection. The word "Abot" in the title of this treatise is used in the sense of chief authorities whose favorite sayings are quoted in this work. On account of the preeminently ethical character of its contents, the treatise is commonly designated as "The Ethics of the Fathers."

14. [1] The Jewish Encyclopedia defines the sefirot as "Potencies or agencies by means of which, according to the Cabala, Elohim manifested His existence in the production of the universe. The term is derived from the Hebrew noun "sefirah," which, meaning originally "number" or "category," alternately assumed in the language of the Zohar the significations of "sphere" (σφαῖρα) and "light" (from סַפִּיר).

15. [1] According to scholars, the Tetragrammaton (or four letters – yod, hey, waw, heh) is the ancient Israelite covenant name for Elohim. It is said that it occurs 5,410 times in the Hebrew Scriptures as the revealed name of the Elohim of Abraham, Isaac and Jacob. It is the name that Yahoshua invoked and shared with his disciples as recorded in John 17.26: "And I have made Your Name known to them, and shall make it known, so that the love with which You loved Me might be in them, and I in them."

16. [1] According to the Jewish Encyclopedia, "...the passage means that if one acts according to the pattern of these middot and shows himself compassionate, merciful, and forgiving toward his fellow creatures, Elohim also will be compassionate and merciful toward him and will forgive his sins (comp. the aphorism of Raba, R. H. 17a, and the remark in Sifre, l.c., that the middot are the ways of Elohim, in which, according to Deut. xi. 22, mankind should walk). In like manner, the words of Rab Judah really denote that if the thirteen middot are the rules of life and conduct, not mere formulas, they will not be inefficacious. The exercise and practise of these virtues cause Elohim to treat man with mercy and compassion, for according to human actions, both in degree and in kind, divine recompense is measured (Soṭah 8b).

17. [1] Exodus 34.6-7: And יהוה passed before him and proclaimed, "יהוה יהוה, an Ěl compassionate and showing favor, patient, and great in kindness and truth, watching over kindness for thousands, forgiving crookedness and transgression and sin, but by no means leaving unpunished, visiting the crookedness of the fathers upon the children and the children's children to the third and the fourth generation."

18. [1] Genesis 1.3 - And Elohim said, "Let light come to be," and light came to be.

19. [1] Exodus 25.1-27.17

20. [1] According to the website Torah.org, Chazal is an acronym for "Chachamim Zichronam Levracham." This means, "Rabbis of blessed memory." If you want a sample then Rabbi Yehudah HaNasi, the codifier of the Mishna is a great example, as well as Rabbi Akiva, whom you may have heard of.

21. According to the Kabbalah Centre, kelipot are "shells created by an individual's negative actions that create a metaphysical barrier between one's self and the Light. Klipot (klipa, singular), which translates from Hebrew as "husks" or "shells," are metaphysical barriers between ourselves and the Light of the Creator that we, ourselves, have created through our own selfish actions. They are what keep us from receiving all the blessings that are meant for us, or from feeling happy, certain, or fulfilled all of the time" (https://www.kabbalah.com/en/articles/klipot/).

22. Isaiah 52.7 - "How pleasant upon the mountains are the feet of him who brings good news, who proclaims peace, who brings good news, who proclaims deliverance, who says to Tsiyon, "Your Elohim reigns!"

23. According to Tania Kotsos's article The Seven Universal Laws Explained from the website Mind Your Reality, she states that the

Law of Correspondence is "the second of the seven Universal Laws is the Law of Correspondence, also known as the Law of Analogy. This Law tells us "As Above So Below, As Below So Above, As Within So Without, As Without So Within". This means that there is "harmony, agreement and correspondence" between the Physical, Mental and Spiritual Planes. Put simply, there is no separation since everything, including you, is Mind. The only difference is the rate of vibration, as the third of the Universal Laws tells us. The same pattern is expressed on all planes of existence from the smallest electron to the largest star, from the visible Physical Plane to the invisible Spiritual Plane (https://mind-your-reality.com/seven_universal_laws.html#part-4).

24. [1] "Man must strive to always keep in mind the thought that everything that he feels comes to him for a purpose from the upper force, from the collective laws of nature. That law brings balance and movement to the physical-biological level, as well as to the spiritual level. You might say that this balance is the return to the center from which we came. Hence, the first condition for keeping this law is to keep in mind the thought that everything I feel comes from one source only, from one center, in order to pull me to it. That law is called the 'law of equivalence of attributes' or the 'law of equivalence of form,' the center, or the Creator." Excerpted from The Law of Equivalence of Attributes from Interview with the Future by Michael Laitman (http://www.kabbalah.info/eng/content/view/frame/4276?/eng/content/view/full/4276&main).

25. Dei Gratia: Lat. By the grace of Elohim. A phrase used in the formal title of a king or queen, importing a claim of sovereignty by the favor or commission of Elohim. In ancient times it was incorporated in the titles of inferior officers, (especially ecclesiastical) but in later use was reserved as an assertion of "the divine right of kings." Black's Law Dictionary. 2nd Edition.

26. Sovereignty: Organized Hypocrisy. Princeton University Press. 1999.

27. [1] According to the Jewish Encyclopedia, Providence "has no equivalent in Biblical Hebrew, the later philosophical writers employing "hashgaḥah" as a translation for the Arabic "'inayah." "Providence" is employed to connote (1) Elohim's "actio æterna" (His foreknowledge and His dispositions for the realization of His supreme will [πρόγνωσις and πρόθεσις]), and (2) Elohim's "actio temporis" (His power to preserve and to control the universe and all that is therein)... Essentially interwoven with the Biblical doctrine of the Messianic kingdom is the thought that the providence of Elohim, the Ruler, is effective in the conflicts and relations of the various peoples. A necessary corollary of this faith in providence was the optimism which characterizes the Biblical world-conception. Evil was either caused by man, who had the freedom of choosing, or was disciplinary and punitive; in either case it served the end of divine providence. https://www.jewishencyclopedia.com/articles/12402-providence#:~:text=Essentially%20interwoven%20with%20the%20Biblical,characterizes%20the%20Biblical%20world%2Dconception.

28. Positive Psychology: An Introduction. M. Seligman & M. Csikszentmihalyi. American Psychologist. January 2000. https://gacbe.ac.in/pdf/ematerial/18BPS6EL-U3.pdf

29. The Amidah is the core of every Jewish worship service, and is therefore also referred to as HaTefillah, or "The prayer." Amidah, which literally means, "standing," refers to a series of blessings recited while standing.

30. Dictionary of Torah Names and Words: Number 8130-8133/8135.

31. According to Quantum Torah's article, The Quantum Leap, "Prior to Creation, there was only the infinite Ohr Ein Sof ("Light of the Infinite") filling all existence. When it arose in Gd's Will to create worlds and emanate the emanated...He contracted ("tzimtzum") Himself in the point at the center, in the very center of His light. He restricted that light, distancing it to the sides surrounding the central point, so that there remained a void, a hollow empty space, away from the central point...After this tzimtzum... He drew down from the Ohr Ein Sof a single straight line [of light] from His light surrounding [the void] from above to below [into the void], and it chained down descending into that void.... In the space of that void He emanated, created, formed and made all the worlds." (Etz Chaim, Heichal A"K, anaf- 2) https://quantumtorah.com/physics-of-tzimtzum-i-the-quantum-leap/

32. "The verb דבר (dabar) means to formalize: to deliberately establish and pronounce something's name or definition. This causes the thing to become "real" in the mind of whoever understands this word, name or definition, and this in turn explains why all of creation was spoken into being, and Man in turn "named" all the animals by their name and finally his Wife by hers (Genesis 2:19-23). This principle sits at the base of nominal reasoning and thus human awareness and ultimately Information. Technology. Noun דבר (dabar) means word. It also means "thing" since the naming of a thing causes the experienced reality of the thing. All thus created "things" together form the whole of experienceable reality, which in turn is called the Word of Elohim." Abarim Publications: https://www.abarim-publications.com/Meaning/Dabar.html

33. Ecclesiastes 3.16 – "He has made it all, pretty in its time. Even the ages He has put in their hearts, except that no one finds out the work that Elohim does from beginning to end."

34. Miracles of Yom Kippur. Rabbi Yossi Laster. Etz Chayim Messianic Synagogue. 2015. https://www.myetzchayim.org/miracles-of-yom-kippur/

35. According the Dictionary of Torah Names and Words, emunah or faith has as an idea that is related to confidence, loyalty, faithfulness, trust, fidelity; training; lit., the force of life flows in unity with purpose and extension; Value 97: [fulfilling] righteous goals.

36. Substantial Evidence Standard. US Legal. https://appeals.uslegal.com/standards-of-review/substantial-evidence-standard/

37. [1] Maimonides states that "by "faith" we do not understand merely that which is uttered with the lips, but also that which is apprehended by the soul, the conviction that the object [of belief] is exactly as it is apprehended. If, as regards real or supposed truths, you content yourself with giving utterance to them in words, without apprehending them or believing in them, especially if you do not seek real truth, you have a very easy task as, in fact, you will find many ignorant people professing articles of faith without connecting any idea with them. If, however, you have a desire to rise to a higher state, viz., that of reflection, and truly to hold the conviction that Elohim is One and possesses true unity, without admitting plurality or divisibility in any sense whatever, you must understand that Elohim has no essential attribute in any form or in any sense whatever, and that the rejection of corporeality implies the rejection of essential attributes." The Guide for the Perplexed. On Faith. Pg. 67.

38. Messianic Consciousness is arrived at when it is through the training of our senses that we are able to discern reality from illusion, truth from falsehood, good from evil. This training that we are to undergo, is nothing less that the discipline found in the Torah. When governed by the Torah, we are able to transcend our worldly, carnal nature and put on the spiritual nature, which is our true self, so as spoken of in the 1st letter to Corinth. This equates to becoming as our Messiah, led by the Torah of יהוה which gives us the authority to manifest the Kingdom of Heaven on Earth. The senses, when refined, therefore, affords us, as our ancestors were able to experience, the ability to have regular, conscious, and intimate encounters with the Spirit of YaH, individually and collectively. Taste and See: Sensing the Spirit by Miykael Qorbanyahu. https://shftngprdgmz.wordpress.com/2020/07/11/taste-and-see-sensing-the-spirit/

39. Matthew 13.11; the secrets of the Torah, or the secrets to the Kingdom of the heavens, entails the revelation of the will of YaH as it relates to the purpose and order of the Kingdom. This revelation is disclosed to those who operate according to the will of YaH as the blessings and promises of YaH are preserved for the faithful members who devote themselves to the study, meditation and application of the Torah. The sages of Israel knew of the secrets of the Torah,

40. [1] "The results of this case-control study suggest that long-term meditators experience enhanced psychosocial wellbeing, such as a better outlook on life experiences and coping skills, a better physical QOL as well as underlying biochemical changes that would contribute to healthy aging…" Impact of Meditation-Based Lifestyle Practices on Mindfulness, Wellbeing, and Plasma Telomerase Levels: A Case-Control Study. N. Dasanayaka N. Sirisena N.Samaranayake. March 2022. https://www.frontiersin.org/journals/psychology/articles/10.3389/fpsyg.2022.846085/full

41. What role does the observer effect play in quantum experiments? Physics Network. December 2023. https://physicsnetwork.org/what-role-does-the-observer-effect-play-in-quantum-experiments.html

42. [1] Embracing uncertainty helps bring order to quantum chaos. The Joint Quantum Institute. September 2023. https://jqi.umd.edu/news/embracing-uncertainty-helps-bring-order-quantum-chaos#:~:text=The%20uncertainty%20principle%20dictates%20that,and%20ergodicity%20challenging%20to%20apply.

43. Neurotheology: The relationship between brain and religion. A. Sayadmansour. National Library of Medicine.2014. https://www.ncbi.nlm.nih.gov/pmc/articles/PMC3968360/#:~:text=%E2%80%9CNeurotheology%E2%80%9D%20refers%20to%20the%20multidisciplinary,the%20human%20brain%20and%20religion.

44. Genesis 17.1-2, Deuteronomy 18.13; Psalm 119.1-2; Proverbs 2.21; Matthew 5.48; Matthew 19.21; 2 Corinthians 13.9-11; 1 John 3.1-10

45. Neuroplasticity. M. Puderbaugh. National Library of Medicine. May 2023. https://www.ncbi.nlm.nih.gov/books/NBK557811/

46. Duties of the Heart. Bachya Ibn Pekudah. Sefaria. https://www.sefaria.org/Duties_of_the_Heart?tab=contents

Made in the USA
Columbia, SC
09 March 2025

54749500R00080